FILLING IN THE GROOVES

THE ULTIMATE GUIDE TO DRUM FILLS

JIM TOSCANO

Edited by Joe Bergamini
Executive Producers: Dom Famularo and Joe Bergamini
Book Design and Layout by Rick Gratton
Music Engraving by Jim Toscano
Cover by Paul Dinovo
All photos and videos courtesy of the author

ONLINE ACCESS INCLUDED

Stream or download the video & audio content for this book.
To access, visit: **alfred.com/redeem**
Enter the following code: 00-47922-118227

WIZDOM MEDIA LLC
48 Troy Hills Rd., Whippany, NJ 07981
Copyright ©2018 Wizdom Media LLC
Exclusively distributed by Alfred Music
No part of this book may be photocopied or reproduced in any way without the prior written consent of the publisher.
Unauthorized uses are an infringement of the US Copyright Act and are punishable by law.

CONTENTS

FOREWORD 5
DRUM KEY/ACKNOWLEDGEMENTS 6
INTRODUCTION/HOW TO USE THIS BOOK 7
THE BACKSTORY 7

Chapter 1 BACK TO BASICS/QUICK START 8

BASIC RHYTHMIC VOCABULARY 9
BACK TO BASICS 10
LESS IS MORE 11
ONE-HIT WONDERS 13
TWO HANDS ARE BETTER THAN ONE 15
BUCKET O'FISH 17

Chapter 2 2ND COURSE 19

SWANGING TRIPLETS 19
DEEP SIXED 21
WALKIN' THE LINE 23
GO FIGURE 25

Chapter 3 THE WHEN 27

MAKING AN ENTRANCE 27
FILLING IN THE MIDDLE 30
YOU'VE CROSSED THE LINE 32

Chapter 4 THE NUMBERS 34

LUCKY SEVEN 34
LUCKY SEVEN WITH A SIDE OF 9 36
MORE IS MORE 38
THINGS HAPPEN IN THREES 40
TAKE FIVE 42
32nd STREET 44
WHEN THINGS GET ODD 46
MORE WITH 24 48
7-6-5-4 50

Chapter 5 RUDIMENTALLY YOURS 52

- CHRONIC FLAMOSIS 52
- KNOW YOUR DIDDLES 54
- WHEN THINGS GET RUFF 56
- LIFE'S A DRAG 58
- FLAMS ON THE DRAG SHELL 60
- A DIDDLE-DIDDLE 62
- RATAMA WHATS? 65
- RUFFIN' THE DRAGS 67

Chapter 6 FUNCTIONS 69

- LAYERED FILLS 67
- SET 'EM UP 71
- DISPLACED NOT MISPLACED 72
- THE BIG ENDING 74
- EXIT STRATEGIES 76

Chapter 7 FOOTNOTES 78

- HOOFS'N'PAWS 78
- MIDDLE FOOT SYNDROME 80
- YOU BE TRIPPIN' 82
- THUNDER FROM DOWN UNDER 84
- LOOK MOM, NO HANDS
  (Fills with Just the Feet) 86
- HAND ME DOWNS 88

Chapter 8 STYLES 90

- LATINISH 90
- DROP ONE IN 92
- NAWLINS STYLE 94
- NAWLINS STYLE PLAY-ALONG 96
- GOT THE BLUES? 97
- GOT THE BLUES? PLAY-ALONG 99
- SHUFFLING ALONG 100
- SHUFFLING ALONG PLAY-ALONG 102
- GET ON THE TRAIN 105
- SWINCOPATION 106
- NOT YOUR GRANDMA'S WALTZ 106
- NOT YOUR GRANDMA'S WALTZ PLAY-ALONG 110
- SIX OR ONE HALF DOZEN 112
- SIX OR ONE HALF DOZEN PLAY-ALONG 114

Chapter 9 HATWORK 116

- YOUR BARK IS WORSE THAN YOUR BITE 116
- AND FOR MY NEXT TRICK, I WILL PULL A FILL OUT OF MY HAT 118
- FILLING IN THE GROOVE 120

Chapter 10 EXTRAS/PLAY-ALONG TRACKS 123

- ONE OF A KIND 124
- WALTZ TO THE WORLD 126
- PUFFS OF SMOKE 128
- SHOOT THE MOON 132

Chapter 11 TRIBUTE 135

- SIMON SAYS / Simon Phillips 135
- GIVE ME LIBERTY / Liberty DeVitto 137
- BONZO BITS / John Bonham 138
- FILL COLLINS / Phil Collins 139
- COBHAM / Billy Cobham 140
- SMITHTOWN / Steve Smith 141
- JEFF PORCARO 142
- OFFICER COPELAND / Stewart Copeland 143
- FORGADDABOUTIT / Steve Gadd 144
- TEN STEPS TO TONY / Tony Williams 145
- RINGO STARR 146
- TODD SUCHERMAN 147
- WHEN NEIL'S AT THE WHEEL / Neil Peart 149
- PORCU-TIME / Gavin Harrison 151

Chapter 8 INDEX/INDEX OF PRACTICE SEGMENTS 153

RESOURCES 160

ABOUT THE AUTHOR 163

ABOUT THE AUDIO AND VIDEO 164

CREDITS 165

FOREWORD

In my global travels of over forty years, I have been very blessed to meet some fantastic drumset artists who inspire people every day with their performance skills. I have also met some incredibly dedicated teachers. Jim Toscano is both.

Jim came to me years ago for lessons and excelled in every session. I was inspired with his endless enthusiasm to learn. He is a natural talent and is a constant learner, and his everyday perseverance is to be studied. It takes this type of person to write a book so clear and exciting that every page is a boost to your creative ability!

Jim talked about the idea for this book many years ago, and was the best person to do the research needed to study all the top drummers and their styles. In these pages, he has captured the basics of drum fills and has discovered a teaching formula for better learning. I am thrilled that Jim has delivered this to the drumming community. In this book, you'll find:

- Great fill suggestions
- Clear transcriptions
- Helpful video and audio tracks
- Exciting play-along songs
- Captured history from the masters

Filling in the Grooves is truly the ultimate guide to drum fills! You will be given top ideas for your creativity to be sparked by studying the masters. Jim has put in the time and effort to start you on a journey of how the best drummers think; how they set up every song with the best fill to emotionally lift the music to the highest level. This is a complete study for all of us to delve into our art form of fills to enhance any musical situation we are playing in. Jim is truly the next generation of great drummers, educators and authors to deliver us a higher understanding of drumset expression!

Now, enjoy ***Filling in the Grooves: The Ultimate Guide to Drum Fills!***

Dom Famularo
Drumming's Global Ambassador

DRUM KEY

Unless otherwise indicated, all examples are in 4/4 time.

ACKNOWLEDGMENTS

I would like to thank everyone who has inspired me to write this book and for the love and support of my family, friends and students! My students are the reason I do what I do.

Thanks to all of my friends in the drumming community for their inspiration and support: Stephane Chamberland, Jason Gianni, Marco Soccoli, Jeff Salem, Memo Acevedo, Paul Cellucci, Joe Testa, Neil Larrivee, Greg Zeller, Chris Stankee, Jojo Mayer, Steve Smith, Billy Cobham, Rod Morgenstein, Joe Franco, Kim Plainfield, Marvin "Smitty" Smith, John Favicchia, Marko Djordjevic, Rodney Howard, Ryan Brown, Jim Riley, and Swiss Chris.

Thanks to all of the talented musicians that have worked on this project with me: Vincent La Russa, Johnny Young, Michelle Young, Calvin Bennet, TJ Jordan, Frank Ferrara, Matthew Schneider, Roger Street Friedman, Steve Uh, Jeff Radke, Jason Wexler, Jason Green, Yanko Valdes, Loic Da Silva, Alberto Toro.

Thank you to Chris Stankee and everyone at Sabian Cymbals, and David Kubes at OffSet pedals for the great products and support!

A special thank you to Rick Gratton for his hard work, time and expertise on the layout of this project.

Thanks to my wife Donna and my daughters Nikki and Lauren for their constant love and support and putting up with the countless hours that I'm hidden away in my studio.

I would like to give special thanks to my teacher and mentor, Dom Famularo and my good friend Joe Bergamini for believing in me and in this project.

INTRODUCTION

This book has been a labor of love for the last five years. I first thought of writing this book because many students would complain that they didn't know what to play when it came to fills. Some students would see me play and ask about how I played a particular fill. I started compiling a list of my own fills. I also looked around and found that although there are countless books on grooves and beats, there really wasn't a comprehensive guide to playing drums fills. I began to develop the idea through teaching my fills to students. Over time, I had compiled 500 of my own fills and over 200 fills from my drum heroes, and so *Filling in the Grooves* was born. There are many more fills that I wasn't able to fit into this book—but I see a Vol. 2 in my future! Writing this book has been such a fun journey for my students and I, since I've tried these fills out on students from all around the globe!

HOW TO USE THIS BOOK

This book is arranged as a series motifs or themes. At the beginning of each theme there is a short introduction to what inspired that particular page. On the corresponding notated page there are a few _practice segments_ that precede the fills. I highly recommend repeating these segments until you have the muscle memory necessary to execute each fill with ease. Pay attention to the stickings and suggested hand movements, but feel free to experiment with your own. I've divided my fills into 52 different pages. I recommend practicing one page a week until you master all of the material over a year—or simply move at your own pace. There are no rules, so feel free to move around the book in any order you like. Use the reference grooves at the beginning of each page so that you can practice the fills in context. Play the grooves in 4- 8- 12- and 16-bar cycles. Play three bars of time and fill on the fourth bar. Play seven bars of time and fill on the eighth bar, etc.

After my fills I've included a tribute section. This section is comprised of transcriptions of fills from some of my drumming heroes that have inspired me throughout my life. I felt that I could have written an endless amount of fills, but I had to narrow down my choices or I'd still be writing this book! At the end of the book I've included an index of all of the practice segments so you can mix, match and create your own.

I sincerely hope that this book serves as a source of inspiration for drummers of all styles and levels. I hope that if you are a teacher you find this to be helpful and fun to explore with your students. I've spent a long time working on it, and it is truly an honor to have someone enjoy the material within these pages.

Filling In The Grooves/Back To Basics

BACK TO BASICS
Quick Start

CHAPTER 1

Think of this page as a salad that is just the lettuce. You've got the bases covered; it just doesn't have all of the toppings or dressing yet. These fills are a great place to start. Tried and true basic fills to get your feet wet! Think Charlie Watts on "Honky Tonk Woman," Ringo Starr on "Day Tripper," Kenny Aronoff on "Pink Houses" or Dave Grohl on "Everlong." These fills are good transition material from one section to another in a song; simple fills that are timeless. You could use this style in a classic rock tune or in a Bruno Mars tune! Simple doesn't have to mean boring; nicely placed accents can emit emotion and just the right feel for a song. Use these fills as a launching pad to create your own fills.

Check out the book *Elements* by John Favicchia for further study

Practice Tips

1. **Count out all of the patterns.**
2. **Play these examples on one surface to get familiar with the pattern.**
3. **Use a metronome, and gradually increase the tempo.**

BACK TO BASICS GROOVE

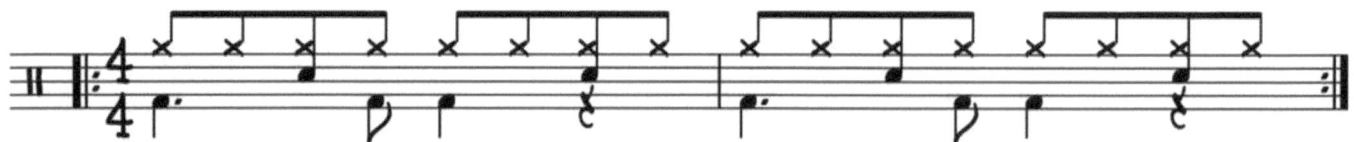

BASIC RHYTHMIC VOCABULARY

PRACTICE SEGMENTS: COMBINE THE FOLLOWING SEGMENTS TO CREATE FILLS OF YOUR OWN

Back To Basics

STRAIGHT ROCK

Jim Toscano and Frank Ferrara

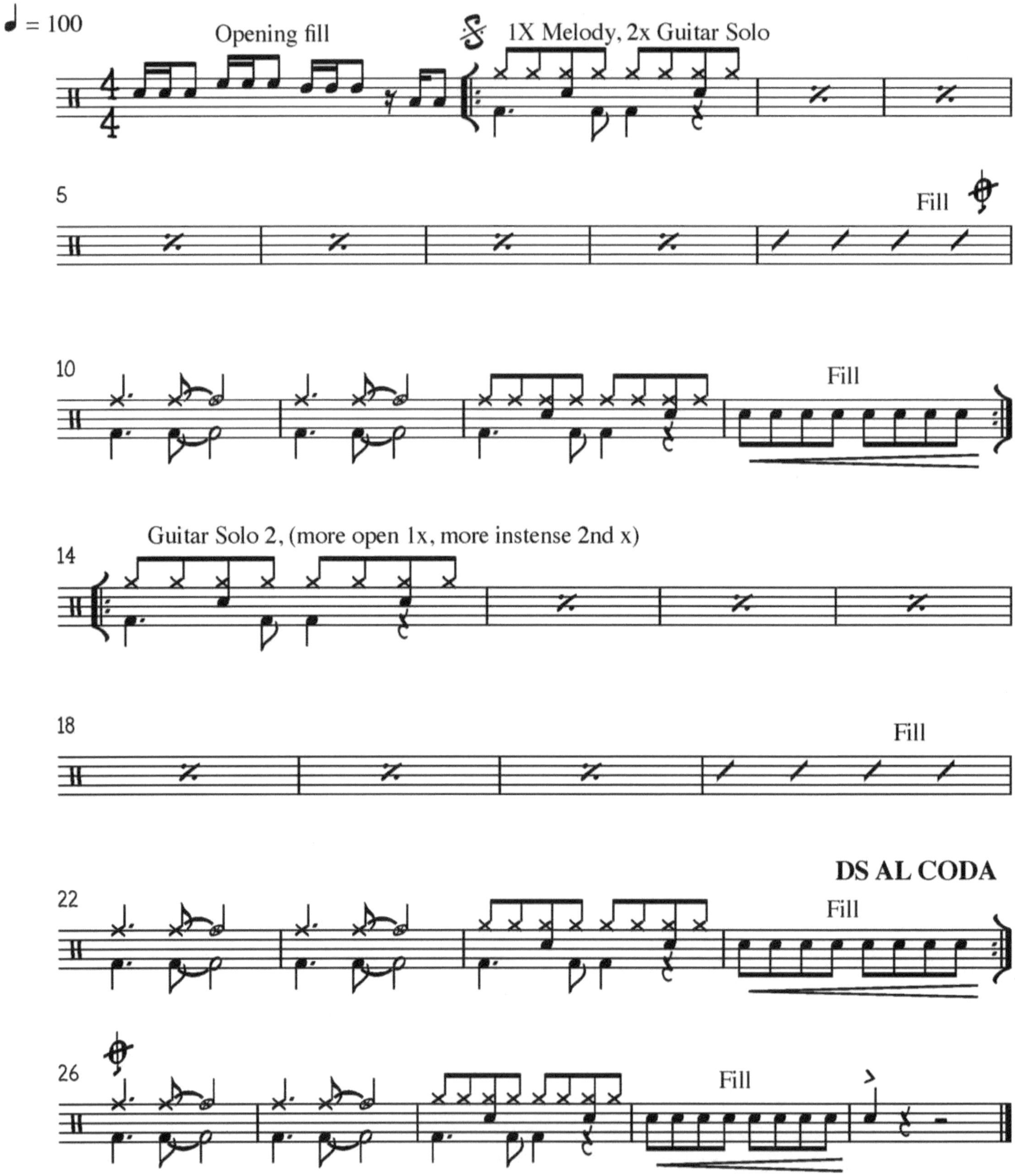

LESS IS MORE

I love a well-placed fill that utilizes space. The space between the notes is just as important as the notes themselves! Sparse fills are non-obtrusive, *play-it-for-the-song* kinds of fills. I use this approach often, because I work for songwriters on a regular basis. When I think of these fills, Russ Kunkel comes to mind, especially on "Fire and Rain" by James Taylor and "North Dakota" by Lyle Lovett. Also check out Carlos Vega on James Taylor's "Copperline," Ringo Starr on The Beatles' "Helter Skelter" and "I Want to Hold Your Hand," and Phil Collins on Genesis' "That's All" and "Follow You Follow Me." Liberty DeVitto's fills in "Summer Highland Falls" by Billy Joel are also some of my favorites. Steve Smith's fill going into the chorus of "Who's Crying Now" by Journey is another great example. I love coming up with fills that use the space around the notes!

Practice Tips

1. Listen to recordings of great songwriters with great drummers!

2. Play with a relaxed feel.

3. Use a metronome and always count.

"LESS IS MORE" GROOVE

LESS IS MORE
SPARSE FILLS

PRACTICE SEGMENTS: COMBINE THE FOLLOWING SEGMENTS TO CREATE FILLS OF YOUR OWN

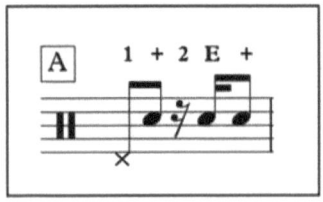
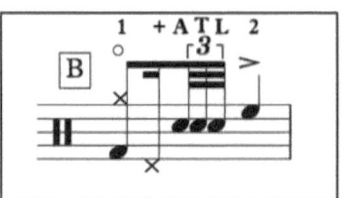
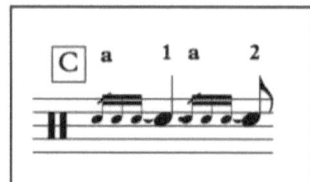

lm #1

lm #2

lm #3

lm #4

lm #5

lm #6

lm #7

lm #8

lm #9

lm #10

ONE-HIT WONDERS

One nicely-placed hit, flam, bark or kick can make a big statement if done right! Think of "The Immigrant Song" by Led Zeppelin: the only fill in the tune is a sixteenth-note snare hit! But without it, the song just wouldn't be the same. Or what about Melvin Parker on "I Got You (I Feel Good)" by James Brown? That single kick hit at the top and the snare hit before each bridge are perfect embellishments to the song. Check out Steve Smith's single flam at the beginning of the second verse of Journey's "Stone in Love," and Simon Phillips' single-note fills on Toto's "Gift of Faith." That's what I'm talking about! These moments can have such a great impact on the listener. The hits below are placed in a variety of spots so you will be ready for any situation.

Practice Tips

1. Listen to the recordings mentioned above.
2. Count out loud.
3. Use a metronome and gradually increase the tempo.

"ONE-HIT WONDERS" BASIC GROOVE

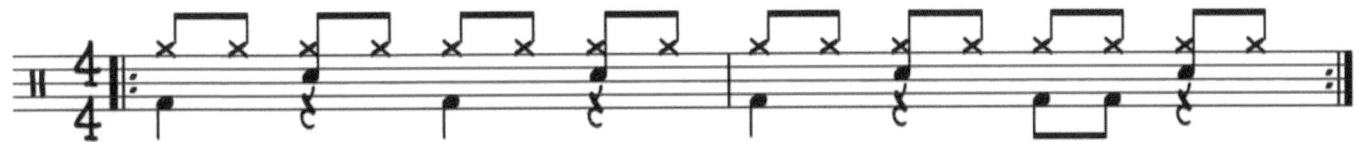

ONE-HIT WONDERS
USING SINGLE-NOTE FILLS TO CREATE SPACE

PRACTICE SEGMENTS: COMBINE THE FOLLOWING SEGMENTS TO CREATE FILLS OF YOUR OWN

TWO HANDS ARE BETTER THAN ONE

This section is all about playing with your hands in unison on two different surfaces. Combinations could include snare and floor tom, snare and hi-hat, snare and cowbell, two different toms, or any other combination of sounds that you like.

For this material I have to again mention my idol, Steve Gadd. I first recognized Steve's use of this concept on Chick Corea's "Samba Song." Also listen to the The New Tony Williams Lifetime track "Snake Oil," Max Roach on "Drums Unlimited" and "Festival Journey," and Louie Bellson's solo work on "Skin Deep" (to name a few). A simple version of this idea would be Ringo Starr's fills on The Beatles' "Drive My Car."

Playing both hands in unison in this manner is sometimes referred to as a *double stop*. I like the feeling and thickness of the sound you get from using two hands. You have to be deliberate yet musical when playing this way, or it can sound overbearing. However, when applied appropriately, there is a very musical aspect to using two hands, and in combination with alternating rhythms you can achieve a wonderful contrast in your playing.

Below is an exercise I use with my students to develop dexterity in this area. I use Ted Reed's *Syncopation* as source material. Play *Syncopation* Set 2 with both hands in unison on two surfaces. Then fill in all of the holes with your bass drum foot as follows:

Ted Reed *Syncopation* Set 2, Ex. 1   Becomes this:

Practice Tips

1. Make sure not to flam—hands are in unison.
2. Play slowly at first.
3. Practice going into a groove and then back to each fill.

"TWO HANDS ARE BETTER THAN ONE" BASIC GROOVE

TWO HANDS ARE BETTER THAN ONE
DOUBLE HANDS

PRACTICE SEGMENTS: COMBINE THE FOLLOWING SEGMENTS TO CREATE FILLS OF YOUR OWN

th #1

32

th #2

33

th #3

34

th #4

35

th #5

36

th #6

37

th #7

38

th #8

39

th #9

40

th #10

41

BUCKET O'FISH

Wow, talk about legendary drum fills! This fill shows up everywhere, from rock to jazz to punk and everywhere in between. It starts songs, ends songs, and can make a big statement. This fill is based on a rudiment called the single-stroke four, and has a bass drum substitution on the "and" of the beat. Practice it with an eighth-note pulse on your metronome.

There are dozens of great recordings to hear this fill in action. An early representation is "Blues for Big Sid" by Max Roach. This fill shows up in many Led Zeppelin/John Bonham tracks, like the guitar solo in "Stairway to Heaven"—and just about every rock drummer from the last five decades has stolen it! Listen to the fills in the Foo Fighters "Times Like These," and for a classic rock version, check out the beginning of "Barracuda" by Heart (Michael DeRosier on drums) and "Double Vision" by Foreigner (Dennis Elliot on drums). This fill also works with 32nd notes and triplets; listen to Steve Smith's 32nd-note version on "Separate Ways" by Journey.

Play through each fill slowly and you will find many uses for this gem.

Practice Tips

1. Play each key segment slowly.

2. Get good separation between the bass drum and toms by listening or try recording yourself.

3. Play with a metronome.

"BUCKET O'FISH" BASIC GROOVE

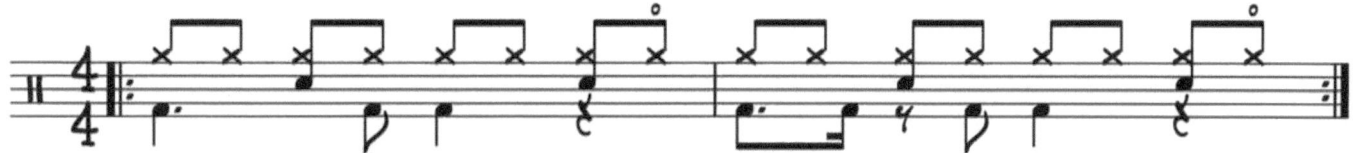

Filling In The Grooves/Back To Basics

BUCKET O'FISH
ONE TRIPLET AND

PRACTICE SEGMENTS: COMBINE THE FOLLOWING SEGMENTS TO CREATE FILLS OF YOUR OWN

Bucket O' Fish and Back

18

CHAPTER 2

2ND COURSE

SWANGING TRIPLETS

This set of fills is based on a specific sticking, so practice the key segments carefully. These fills remind me of swinging big band fills. My fist exposure to big band was when my Dad took me to see Buddy Rich at the Brooklyn Academy of Music in fifth grade. I got home that night and couldn't put my sticks down! To hear this concept, check out "Mexicali Nose" from *Buddy Live at Birdland* and Louie Bellson's "Seven Come Eleven." I eventually recognized its use in rock, blues, R&B and hip-hop as well. One such track is Joe Jackson's "Sunday Papers" with David Houghton on drums.

I use it in most styles of music, as long as there is a swing in the groove and it's in the right tempo range (85-130 BPM). It's fun to play, rolls off of your hands easily, is effective in solos, and works well on the hi-hat during half-time shuffles.

Practice Tips

1. Learn the sticking pattern.
2. Pay attention to the accents.
3. Play with a metronome.

BASIC GROOVE FOR "SWANGIN TRIPLETS"
(PUT A LITTLE SWING ON IT)

SWANGING TRIPLETS

PRACTICE SEGMENTS: COMBINE THE FOLLOWING SEGMENTS TO CREATE FILLS OF YOUR OWN

DEEP SIXED

The six-stroke roll is one of the PAS 40 International Drum Rudiments. It's commonly written as a sixteenth-and 32nd-note rhythm, but as a triplet figure it works great and rolls off the hands very easily. The use of six-stroke rolls in fills goes back to early R&B and Motown. In fact, the "Motown fill" can be played with a closed five- or six-stroke roll. I prefer the latter. Richard "Pistol" Allen from Motown's Funk Brothers in-house band played this fill on many legendary tracks. Listen to the intro of "My Girl" and "I Can't Help Myself (Sugar Pie Honey Bunch)." An early inspiration of mine, and a recording containing these ideas is Joe Jackson's *Look Sharp*, with David Houghton on drums, especially the song "Is She Really Going Out with Him" and the drum break in the title track.

This sticking is also common in jazz and fusion. Check out Steve Smith on Vital Information's "One Flight Up" (from *Vitalive!*), and Dennis Bradford on "Wizard Island" by The Jeff Lorber Fusion.

I learned this riff as a young drummer and have used it in many different ways since then. It is a great connecting fill between sections of songs. Achieving a smooth flow is *most* important. Practice the written rudiment until it feels good. Make sure to accent the first and last note. The Moeller method will make playing this rudiment most efficient. Play through all of the fills and before long you will be creating your own.

Practice Tips

1. **Practice the rudiment until it flows.**

2. **Learn the sticking and memorize it.**

3. **Use upstrokes and downstrokes to produce good accents.**

BASIC GROOVE FOR "DEEP SIXED" (SLIGHT SWING)

BASIC GROOVE WITH GHOST NOTES

DEEP SIXED

PRACTICE SEGMENTS: COMBINE THE FOLLOWING SEGMENTS TO CREATE FILLS OF YOUR OWN

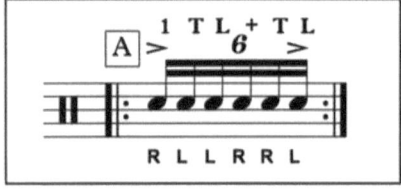

WALKIN' THE LINE

The fills on this page are meant to feel like grooves. The term "linear" refers to a musical line where no notes overlap (i.e., no two limbs play at the same time). It also refers to a style of drumming. Two books that influenced me early on in this style were *The Funk Drumming Workbook* by my good friend Chet Doboe and *Advanced Funk Studies* by Rick Latham. Also make sure to check out *Future Sounds* by David Garibaldi for further study.

My inspiration for this page comes from listening to grooves played by many of my drumming heroes. Steve Gadd is a master of this approach. Check out his brilliant linear patterns on Chick Corea's "Lenore," and Lee Ritenour's "French Roast." David Garibaldi's playing is almost synonymous with the style. Check out "If I Play My Cards Right" and "On The Serious Side" from Tower of Power. Simon Phillips is also a master of this approach; listen to his playing on the Toto track "I Will Remember" (from *Tambu*) and the Los Lobotomys song "Party in Simon's Pants" (from *Candyman*). Another great example is "U.S. Drag" by Missing Persons, with Terry Bozzio on drums.

This style of fill provides a lift to connect sections, and provides rhythmic excitement that differs from the groove, but keeps strong time and therefore momentum. These fills also have a unique dynamic shape. The hi-hat plays "in between the cracks," or between the snare and tom hits. Most of these fills are executed open-handed (hands not crossed). If you are not accustomed to playing this way, this page will provide a good platform to practice this concept and hopefully inspire fills and grooves of your own.

Practice Tips

1. **Play each key segment open-handed until you are comfortable.**
2. **Count sixteenth notes out loud in 4/4 time.**
3. **Play with a metronome!**

BASIC LINEAR GROOVE

WALKIN' THE LINE
LINEAR FILLS

PRACTICE SEGMENTS: COMBINE THE FOLLOWING SEGMENTS TO CREATE FILLS OF YOUR OWN

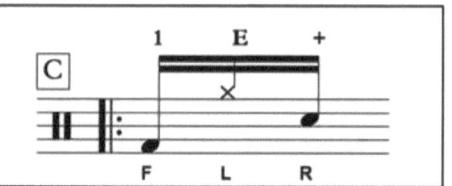

GO FIGURE

Understanding common figures in music is an important job for the drummer. A *figure* refers to a musical phrase played by the entire band, an ensemble figure or a phrase played by part of the band, or a section figure. Section figures are usually notated above the regular staff, and an ensemble figure is typically notated on the snare space on the staff.

It's not only about playing the figure, but interpreting the phrase being played by the band. This section is a simple guide to some very common musical phrases. I can remember when I was a kid studying drums, being handed big band charts and not really getting a good explanation as to what the figures were about, or what to do with them. There was no YouTube to look up examples; I was on my own to figure it out. It wasn't until I started doing theater work that I began to understand the concept. I hope this section sheds a little light on this concept.

For some great listening, check out Bob Mintzer's track "Elvin's Mambo" with Peter Erskine on drums. The album *Wizard Island* by The Jeff Lorber Fusion, with Dennis Bradford on drums, is filled with ensemble work. Listen to Dave Weckl's playing on "Why Not" by Michel Camilo and Buddy Rich's drumming on "Straight No Chaser" from the album *A Different Drummer*.

Check out the book *Elements* by John Favicchia for further study, and for big band practice check out *I've Got You Under My Skins* by Irv Cottler.

Practice Tips

1. **Listen to the recordings mentioned above.**
2. **Always be aware of the time through the figure.**
3. **Count out loud.**

"GO FIGURE" BASIC GROOVE

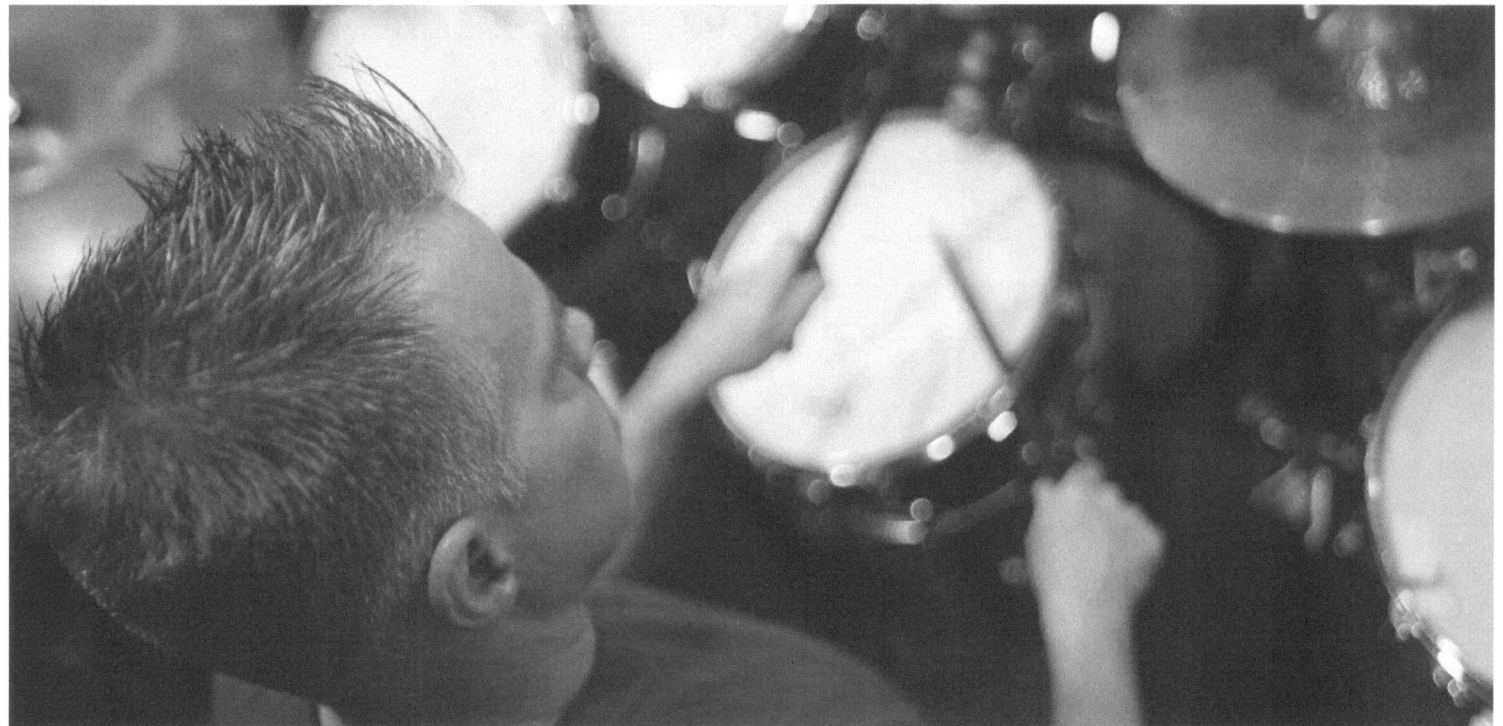

GO FIGURE
FILLS AROUND COMMON ROCK FIGURES

PRACTICE SEGMENTS: COMBINE THE FOLLOWING SEGMENTS TO CREATE FILLS OF YOUR OWN

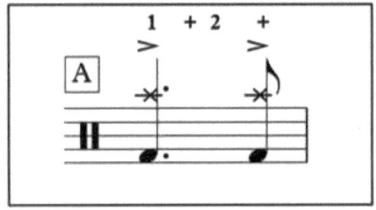

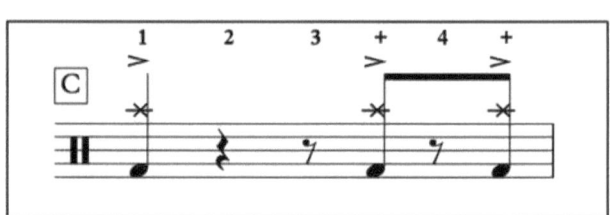

gf #1

82

gf #2
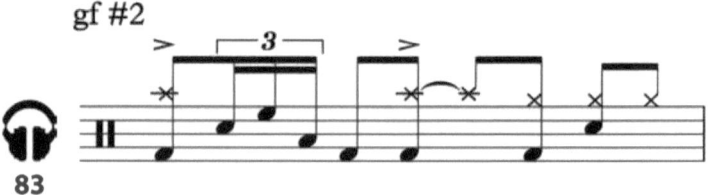
83

gf #3

84

gf #4

85

gf #5

86

gf #6

87

gf #7

88

gf #8
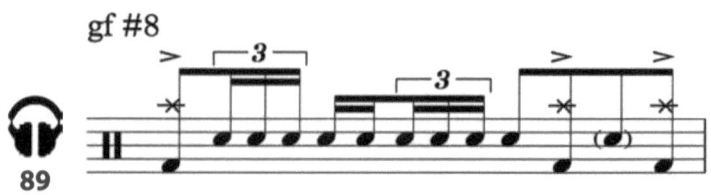
89

gf #9

90

gf #10

91

CHAPTER 3

THE WHEN

MAKING AN ENTRANCE

A great fill at the beginning of a song can be effective and instantly recognizable. Think of Bonham's fill at the beginning of "D'yer Mak'er" by Led Zeppelin or Liberty DeVitto's fill at the beginning of "Only the Good Die Young" or "Uptown Girl" by Billy Joel. Another iconic fill is at the beginning of "Rock with You" by Michael Jackson, with John Robinson on drums. Phil Collins does a nice job playing simple and effective intros that setup the groove really well, like the fill at the beginning of "Inside Out." Also listen to Neil Peart's fill on the intro of Rush's "Digital Man."

Listen to your favorite recording and notice how some of your favorite players set up a song. The set up fill can be vital in setting the mood of a particular song!

I tried to provide a few fills that work at the top of a tune. These fills are very simple, yet effective. You've probably heard some of these ideas before.

Practice Tips

1. **Play each fill, then play the suggested groove at the appropriate tempo.**
2. **Get good separation between the notes.**
3. **Practice with a metronome.**

"MAKING AN ENTRANCE" BASIC GROOVE

MAKING AN ENTRANCE

FILLS TO START SONGS OR ENTER FROM SECTIONS WHERE TIME HAS STOPPED

SOME FAMOUS DRUMMERS "MAKING AN ENTRANCE"

PHIL COLLINS

"Something Happened on the Way to Heaven"

"Inside Out"

JOHN BONHAM

"Moby Dick"

"D'yer Mak'er"

JEFF PORCARO

"Hold the Line"

"Rosanna"

STEWART COPELAND

"Can't Stand Losing You"

"Driven to Tears"

RINGO STARR

"Birthday"

"Savoy Truffle"

LIBERTY DeVITTO

"Allentown"

"Only the Good Die Young" (brushes)

FILLING IN THE MIDDLE

I use this type of fill often. It's kind of like a plastic Easter egg with candy in the middle! The basic idea is to groove on 1 and 4 and play your fill on beats 2 and 3, thus keeping the backbeat present. What's nice about this kind of fill is that the groove is not interrupted, and the momentum continues forward. I like using this type of fill with songwriters in the folk-rock genre, as it doesn't take away from the song. Listen to guys like Russ Kunkel, Carlos Vega, and Jim Keltner. A couple specific songs that use this concept brilliantly are "That Voice Again" by Peter Gabriel (Manu Katche on drums) and "My Secret Place" by Joni Mitchell. It is also quite common in funk and R&B drumming as well. These fills provide a sneaky place for creative ideas!

Practice Tips

1. Make sure to keep an even flow.
2. Play strong backbeats on 2 and 4.
3. Practice with a metronome.

"FILLING IN THE MIDDLE" BASIC GROOVE

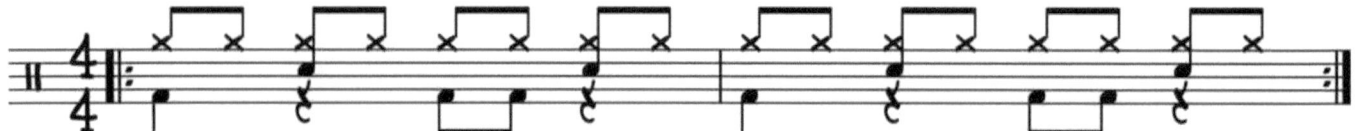

FILLING IN THE MIDDLE
FILLS IN THE MIDDLE OF TIME

PRACTICE SEGMENTS: COMBINE THE FOLLOWING SEGMENTS TO CREATE FILLS OF YOUR OWN

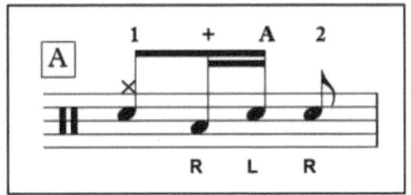

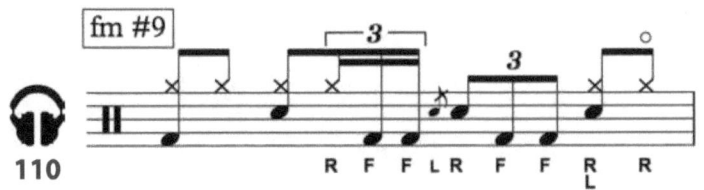

31

YOU'VE CROSSED THE LINE

Over-the-barline fills create tension in a very interesting way. They are not at all predictable, and they add a new level of excitement to the music. I'm not talking about two-bar fills; I'm talking about starting a fill on beat 3 of one bar and playing into beat 2 of the next bar! Just make sure that your time is solid and that it's played in music that asks for this approach. It probably won't fly in a squeaky clean pop tune—but when it works, it is very exciting. For a rock example, check out "Monkey Wrench" by the Foo Fighters with Dave Grohl on drums. I also love Neil Peart's over-the-bar fills in the ending of "Big Money" by Rush, and the fills on Steely Dan's "Bad Sneakers", with Jeff Porcaro on drums. Also listen to "You Know What I Mean" by Jeff Beck, with Richard Bailey on drums, and Stewart Copeland with The Police on "Driven to Tears."

I find playing through beat 1 of the following bar is not only functional for setting up figures, but it's also interesting and fun!

Practice Tips

1. Practice slowly and count.
2. Play with a relaxed feel.
3. Practice with a metronome.

"YOU'VE CROSSED THE LINE" BASIC GROOVE

Filling In The Grooves/The When

YOU'VE CROSSED THE LINE
FILLING OVER THE BAR LINE

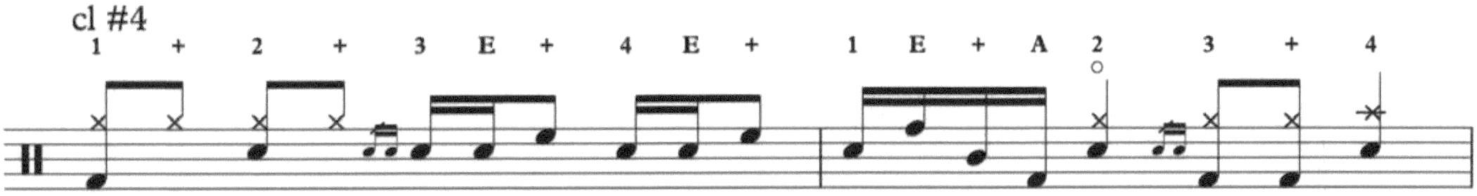

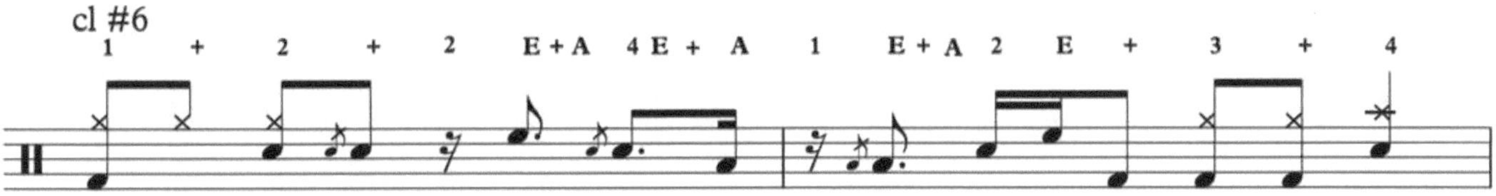

CHAPTER 4

THE NUMBERS

LUCKY SEVEN

I wrote this section to give a simple guide to approaching fills in 7/8 time. Many students can get a simple 7 groove together, but then have a hard time trying to execute fills that work and feel good as well. Although it is one of the most common "odd"-time signatures, 7/8 is still not the norm for Western music. Our culture does not easily feel this time, and we certainly do not dance in 7. The folk songs of Bulgaria, Romania, and Greece are commonly in 7. People dance to this music there because it originates in the folk music of these cultures.

If you subdivide a bar of 7 into 2+2+3, 3+2+2, 4+3, or 3+4, it is much easier to feel and count than if you counted to 7. Use this page as an intro to playing and filling in 7. Some genres to hear odd times are progressive rock, fusion, and classical music. Listen to Terry Bozzio on "Pound for a Brown" by Frank Zappa, whose use of odd times is legendary. Also check out Neil Peart's playing on "Subdivisions" and "Natural Science" from Rush. "Biplane to Bermuda," from Simon Phillips' album *Symbiosis*, is one of the many examples of great odd-time tracks from him. If you like progressive rock and metal, bands like Tool and Dream Theater provide a nice palette of odd-time ideas.

For further study in this area, check out the book *Odd Feelings* by Massimo Russo with Dom Famularo.

Practice Tips

1. **Practice counting in 7 and identify the subdivisions.**
2. **Play with a metronome.**
3. **When counting, say "sev," not "sev-en" (which has two syllables).**

BASIC 7/8 GROOVE

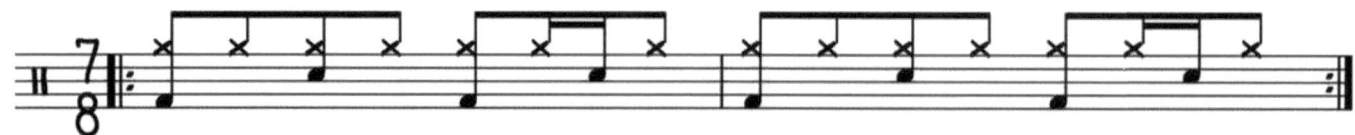

7/8 GROOVE FROM PLAY-ALONG

LUCKY 7
FILLS IN 7/8 TIME

PRACTICE SEGMENTS: COMBINE THE FOLLOWING SEGMENTS TO CREATE FILLS OF YOUR OWN

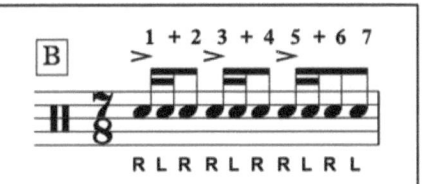
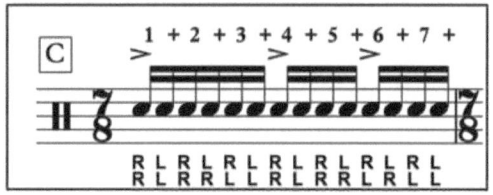

L7 #1

118

L7 #2

119

L7 #3
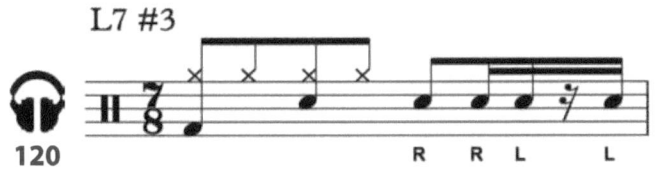
120

L7 #4

121

L7 #5

122

L7 #6

123

L7 #7

124

L7 #8

125

L7 #9

126

L7 #10

127

LUCKY 7 WITH A SIDE OF 9

128

♩=110

JIM TOSCANO

MORE IS MORE

This area is all about the fill! "More is more" is not the approach to take on a James Taylor track or a nice ballad—*you will* get fired! This type of treatment is "soloistic" and fits well in more aggressive music, instrumental music, progressive rock, metal, etc. The first drummer that comes to mind for me in this section is Billy Cobham. Billy was able to squeeze an incredible flurry of notes into small spaces—but with power and intention. Listen to Billy on the tracks "Vital Transformation" (on the Mahavishnu Orchestra's *Inner Mounting Flame*) and "Stratus" (on Cobham's *Spectrum*). Terry Bozzio is another madman in this area, as heard in his work on "Danger Money" by UK and "Sponge" by the Brecker Brothers. More recently, Virgil Donati, on the *Universe* album by Planet X, and Matt Garska, with Animals as Leaders on tracks like "Mind-Spun" and "Thoroughly at Home," have been pushing this type of drumming to new heights!

Practice Tips

1. Break down each fill into small components.

2. Play slowly and count!

3. Use a metronome and gradually increase the tempo.

"MORE IS MORE" GROOVE

MORE IS MORE
VERY BUSY FILLS

PRACTICE SEGMENTS: COMBINE THE FOLLOWING SEGMENTS TO CREATE FILLS OF YOUR OWN

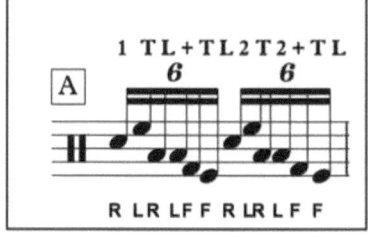

mm #1

130

mm #2

131

mm #3

132

mm #4

133

mm #5

134

mm #6

135

mm #7

135

mm #8

136

mm #9

137

mm #10

138

THINGS HAPPEN IN THREES

I love the feeling of three against four. This section is based on this common cross-rhythm/polyrhythm. I call it common because most musicians can feel this immediately. It has origins in African folk music, and can be heard in Afro-Cuban music as well. You can think of this rhythm as cross-rhythmic threes, meaning the rhythmic pattern is based on the dotted eighth-note pulse. I start the cycle on the 1 or the upbeat of 1. The patterns in this section have one sticking that has been expanded to several orchestrations. This can also be categorized as "ruffs in three." For our purposes, I am defining a ruff as two single grace notes. This strategy provides tension in the music, resulting in an exciting musical event. You will hear these patterns in famous fills by the likes of Neil Peart, Simon Phillips and, more recently, by such drummers as Gavin Harrison (for example, on the track "Centered" by Gavin Harrison and 05Ric).

Practice Tips

1. Go through each of the practice segments carefully.
2. Play with a relaxed feel.
3. Use a metronome and gradually increase the tempo.

"THINGS HAPPEN IN THREES" BASIC GROOVE

Filling In The Grooves/The Numbers

THINGS HAPPEN IN THREES
ACCENT EVERY THREE SIXTEENTHS

PRACTICE SEGMENTS: COMBINE THE FOLLOWING SEGMENTS TO CREATE FILLS OF YOUR OWN

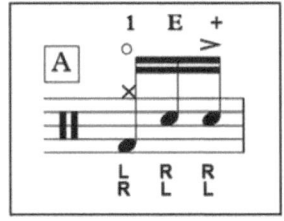 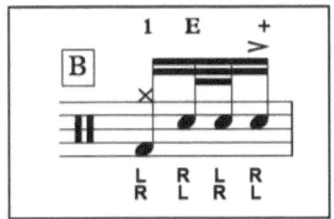 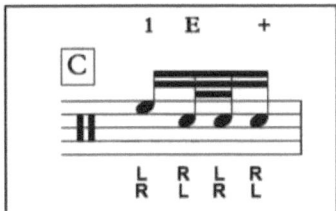 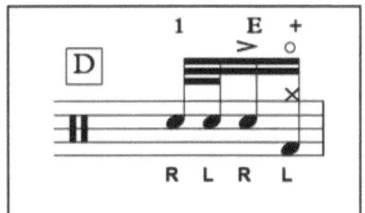

tt #1

139

tt #2

140

tt #3

141

tt #4

142

tt #5

143

tt #6

144

tt #7

tt #8

145

tt #9

146

tt #10

147

41

Filling In The Grooves/The Numbers

TAKE FIVE

This section is all about fives! I'm not necessarily talking about playing in five, although that does have an incredible drumset history. The Dave Brubeck composition "Take Five," which is a 5/4 "jazz waltz," was recorded in 1959. The legendary Joe Morello played a beautiful musical solo on this tune, one of the most famous in jazz. However, here I used the title as a metaphor about playing cross-rhythms grouped in five, as well as quintuplets. I love the sound of fives, the feeling of them, and the interesting character they lend to music! Fives can create tension in the music, and lead the listener to believe that the pulse sounds odd or random—then to arrive back solidly on the one!

My introduction to this topic was very early on, playing through etudes from *Portraits in Rhythm* by Anthony Cirone, and hearing my father play Stravinsky's "The Rite of Spring" for me. Later, I discovered the music of Frank Zappa with his use of fives. All of these sources have drawn me to study this material. Be careful how you use it! It's not for every situation, but I provided a sprinkling of ideas.

Listen to Vinnie Colaiuta on "Spokes" by Alan Holdsworth, Terry Bozzio on "Some Skunk Funk" by the Brecker Brothers, Steve Gadd on "Fawlty Tenors" by Steps Ahead, and Ralph Humphrey on "Zombie Woof" by Frank Zappa for inspiration on this topic!

Practice Tips

1. Listen to the recordings mentioned above.

2. Count out all of the patterns.

3. Play these examples on one surface to get familiar with the pattern.

4. Use a metronome and gradually increase the tempo.

"TAKE FIVE" BASIC GROOVE

42

TAKE FIVE
QUINTUPLETS AND CROSS-RHYTHMIC FIVES

PRACTICE SEGMENTS: COMBINE THE FOLLOWING SEGMENTS TO CREATE FILLS OF YOUR OWN

USE THE FOLLOWING SYLLABLES TO COUNT THE QUINTUPLETS: 1 E AN DA LA

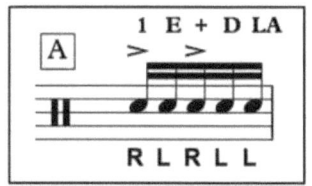

tf #1 — 148

tf #2 — 149

tf #3 — 150

tf #4 — 151

tf #5 — 152

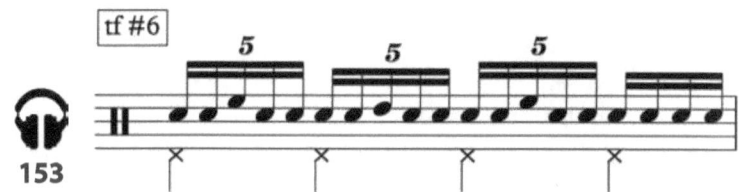

tf #6 — 153

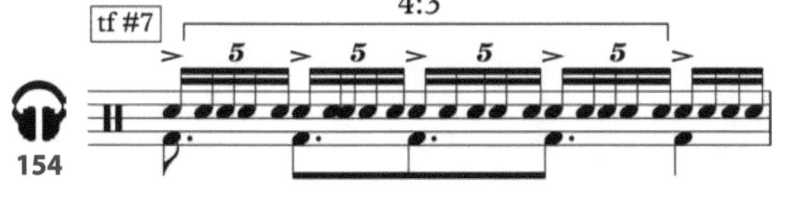

tf #7 — 154

tf #8 — 155

tf #9 — 156

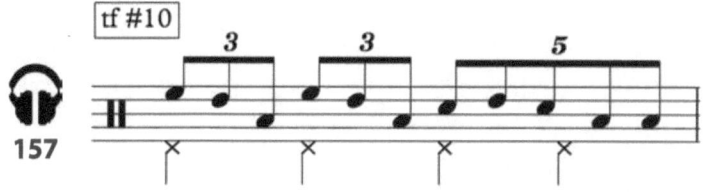

tf #10 — 157

32nd STREET

Students often ask me about how to use 32nd notes—and more importantly, how to count them. The first thing is to realize that you need four notes per eighth note, and eight notes per quarter note. While counting sixteenth notes out loud, play two notes per sixteenth note for each syllable (1 e & a). Practice playing a bar of sixteenth notes, then a bar of 32nd notes. Use a metronome with a quarter-note pulse, as well as an eighth-note pulse, in order to feel both eight- and four-note subdivisions. This check pattern will help you establish the time and feeling of the 32nd notes.

My first influence in this area would have to be Billy Cobham on "Stratus," followed by Simon Phillips' use of 32nd-note rolls in some of his solos. The two drum solos on the *Simon Phillips Complete* DVD (Alfred) are great examples.

Practice Tips

1. **Practice the 16th-to-32nd- note check pattern mentioned above.**

2. **Count out all of the patterns using an eighth-note pulse.**

3. **Play these examples on one surface to get familiar with the patterns.**

4. **Use a metronome and gradually increase the tempo.**

"32nd STREET" BASIC GROOVE

32nd STREET
FILLS USING 32ND NOTES

PRACTICE SEGMENTS: COMBINE THE FOLLOWING SEGMENTS TO CREATE FILLS OF YOUR OWN

= R CROSSES OVER L

WHEN THINGS GET ODD

These fills utilize odd-number groupings in cross-rhythms. I've bracketed the groups so you have a clear picture of how they are assembled. This is just a basic approach to this material; for further study check out Gary Chaffee's *Patterns* books. Odd groupings give an interesting rhythmic landscape to your fills, but you have to be comfortable hearing the quarter-note pulse in this context, or you run the risk of crashing the band. You have to know where you are at all times! Practice this material slowly, with a metronome. Some great examples of this type of playing can be found by listening to Vinnie Colaiuta with Allan Holdsworth, Gavin Harrison with 05Ric, and Mike Mangini with Dream Theater.

Practice Tips

1. Listen to the recordings from the drummers mentioned above.

2. Count out all of the patterns.

3. Play these examples on one surface to get familiar with the pattern.

4. Use a metronome and gradually increase the tempo.

"WHEN THINGS GET ODD" BASIC GROOVE

WHEN THINGS GET ODD
FILLS USING ODD-NUMBERED GROUPINGS

PRACTICE SEGMENTS: COMBINE THE FOLLOWING SEGMENTS TO CREATE FILLS OF YOUR OWN

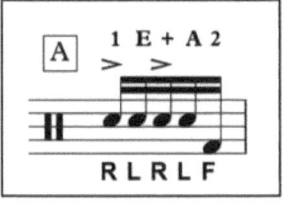
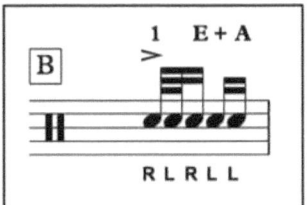

MORE WITH 24

This section explores the use of cross-rhythms in sixteenth-note triplets. I became interested in this concept originally from listening to early jazz recordings where the triplets were being grouped in twos and fours. Then I decided to explore it further, and wrote an extensive lesson on the subject. This is just a sampling of the topic.

Billy Cobham and Simon Phillips come to mind when working on this concept. Check out Simon's playing on "Spark" and "Move" by Hiromi, and Billy Cobham's fill before the outro of "Mozaik" from the album *Warning*.

Practice Tips

1. Play each sticking until you feel comfortable.
2. Use a metronome set to eighth notes.
3. Play slowly and count out loud.

"MORE WITH 24" BASIC GROOVE

MORE WITH 24
ADVANCED PHRASING USING SIXTEENTH-NOTE TRIPLETS

Basic four-note subdivision

Basic four-note subdivision (2 accents)

Basic four-note subdivision (paradiddles)

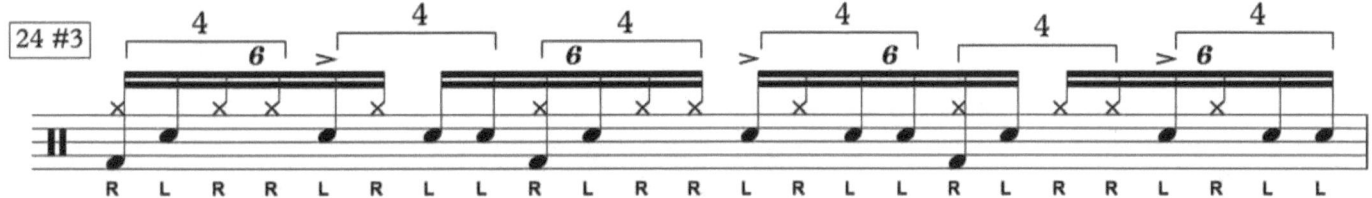

Basic five-note and four-note subdivisions in (5,4,5,4,6)

Sevens simple orchestration

7-6-5-4

This section is from a study I started working on years ago. My intention was to make odd-numbered groupings more user-friendly. My inspiration for this page comes from listening to the music of Frank Zappa, with the likes of Terry Bozzio, Vinnie Colaiuta, Ralph Humphrey, and Chad Wackerman on drums. Frank Zappa's "The Black Page Drum Solo" was written with Terry Bozzio in mind, and took odd groupings to another level. Terry knocked it out of the park! I'm also intrigued by how Vinnie Colaiuta uses these groupings so effortlessly in his fills, like in the opening fill on "Spokes" from Alan Holdsworth.

For further study, check out *It's Your Move* by Dom Famularo and Joe Bergamini, and the *Patterns* series by Gary Chaffee.

Practice Tips

1. Practice these fills on one surface with a metronome.
2. Play through the practice segments slowly.
3. Use "1, e, an, da, la" for counting quintuplets.
4. Use "1, e, an, e, an, da, la" for counting septuplets.
5. Count out loud.

"7-6-5-4" BASIC GROOVE

7-6-5-4
FILLS USING SEPTUPLETS AND QUINTUPLETS WITH SIX-STROKE ROLLS AND SIXTEENTH NOTES

PRACTICE SEGMENTS: COMBINE THE FOLLOWING SEGMENTS TO CREATE FILLS OF YOUR OWN

CHAPTER 5: RUDIMENTALY YOURS

CHRONIC FLAMOSIS

I love the use of flams in fills. Flams are meant to effectively elongate a note. They can add emphasis and musicality. From the most simple flam-on-4 fill (brah!) or flam-kick (brah, goom) to Swiss army triplets (brah-ga-da), the flam is a must when creating punchy fills with finesse and flare! Try all of the flam rudiments on the kit. You will have a blast!

Tony Williams' use of flams is legendary and helped define his style; listen to the Tony Williams Lifetime records. I love the way Steve Gadd uses flams on the track "Samba Song" by Chick Corea. Gavin Harrison's flam fills on "Blackest Eyes" by Porcupine Tree are modern and powerful. This treatment will never get old and changes the fill by adding a slightly technical aspect to it. For further study in flams, check out the section entitled Flam Intervention from *It's Your Move* by Dom Famularo and Joe Bergamini.

Practice Tips
1. Learn the sticking pattern.
2. Pay attention to the accents.
3. Be sure not to play flat flams or double stops.

"CHRONIC FLAMOSIS" BASIC GROOVE

CHRONIC FLAMOSIS
FILLS WITH FLAMS

PRACTICE SEGMENT: COMBINE THE FOLLOWING SEGMENTS TO CREATE FILLS OF YOUR OWN

cf #1

182

cf #2

183

cf #3

184

cf #4

185

cf #5

186

cf #6

187

cf #7

188

cf #8

189

cf #9

190

cf #10

191

KNOW YOUR DIDDLES

This section is based on our good friend the paradiddle, the one rudiment that most musicians—even non-drummers—have heard of. *Stick Control* by George Lawrence Stone (starting with exercises 5-8 on page 5) can provide an amazing platform for getting these ideas together. The paradiddle provides equal opportunity for the left and right to lead. Moving accents through this rudiment provides great phrasing. The paradiddle is also used as a turning stroke to switch leading hands. I've placed accents in spots that create figures that have a great feel and almost function as grooves themselves!

Check out Steve Gadd's playing on "Fawlty Tenors" from the Steps Ahead album *Smokin' the Pit* to hear some of his signature use of diddles. Sources that provide great further study are the book *Advanced Concepts* by Kim Plainfield and the *Methods and Mechanics* DVD by Todd Sucherman.

Practice Tips

1. If you haven't already, memorize this rudiment!
2. Practice the accent patterns.
3. At first, play on a practice pad and use a metronome.

"KNOW YOUR DIDDLES" BASIC GROOVE

KNOW YOUR DIDDLES
FILLS USING PARADIDDLES

PRACTICE SEGMENTS: COMBINE THE FOLLOWING SEGMENTS TO CREATE FILLS OF YOUR OWN

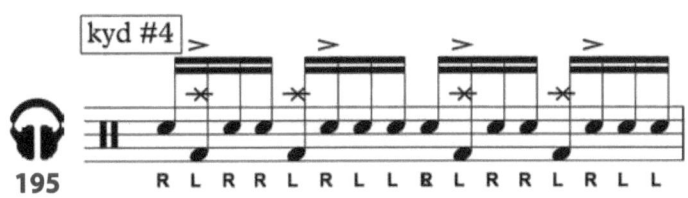

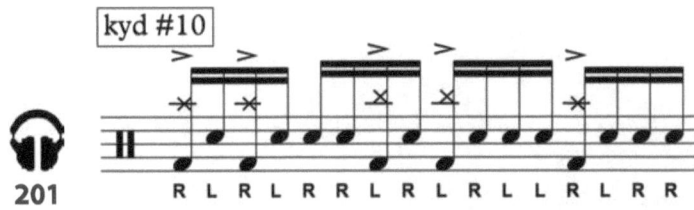

55

WHEN THINGS GET RUFF

This section uses ruffs in odd groupings to provide rhythmic variety to our fills. Kim Plainfield first introduced me to this concept at Drummers Collective, with his exercise "odd ruffs." Neil Peart's playing on "The Spirit of Radio" by Rush is filled with figures using this concept. You can hear some nice examples of this on "Indian Summer" from Simon Phillips' *Symbiosis* album. Also listen to Michel Camilo's "On Fire" and "Just Kidding" with Dave Weckl on drums. But this concept is not new. You can hear these elements in fills and solos by Elvin Jones and Tony Williams in the jazz idiom, and countless other drummers in the jazz, fusion, and rock worlds. Play through the key segments, and practice them with a metronome to make sure you are always aware of the quarter-note pulse. The bass drum substitutions can be challenging, but very exciting in context.

For further study, check out the "odd ruffs" section of *Advanced Concepts* by Kim Plainfield and the exercises in *It's Your Move* by Dom Famularo and Joe Bergamini.

Practice Tips

1. **Listen to the recordings mentioned above until you hear and understand the concepts.**
2. **Play with a relaxed feel.**
3. **Use a metronome and gradually increase the tempo.**

"WHEN THINGS GET RUFF" BASIC GROOVE

WHEN THINGS GET RUFF
MORE FILLS WITH RUFFS

PRACTICE SEGMENTS: COMBINE THE FOLLOWING SEGMENTS TO CREATE FILLS OF YOUR OWN

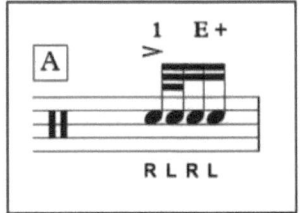
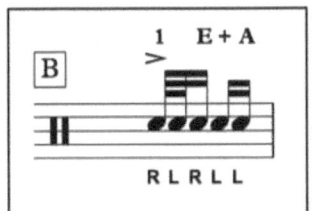
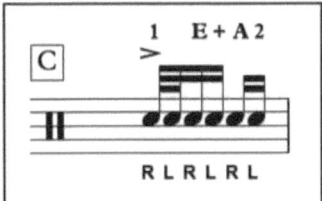

gr #1

202

gr #2

203

gr #3

204

gr #4

205

gr #5

206

gr #6

207

gr #7

208

gr #8

209

gr #9

210

gr #10

211

LIFE'S A DRAG

Fills utilizing drags have a certain finesse and nuance. They can provide a slightly syrupy feel at slower tempos, and can add excitement at fast tempos.

People often debate the differences between drags and ruffs. For my purposes, the drag is defined as a pair of grace notes played with a double stroke, where as the ruff is a pair (or more) of grace notes played with single strokes. Practicing this rudiment provides an important skill that every drummer should master. This includes hand-to-hand drags, as well as all of the drag rudiments.

I first became interested in the use of drags in my younger years, listening to my favorite jazz drummers like Buddy Rich, Max Roach, Louie Bellson, and Art Blakey. The drag is so pronounced in the music they were playing. The Steely Dan tracks "Dirty Work" and "Reelin' in the Years," with Jim Hodder on drums, provide some nice examples of fills with drags. "The Royal Scam" also has some tasty drag fills, with Bernard Purdie on drums. Two great Jeff Beck tracks for drag fills are "Air Blower" from *Blow by Blow* (Richard Bailey on drums) and "Led Boots" from *Wired* (Narada Michael Walden on drums).

Practice Tips

1. Work on drag rudiments from the P.A.S. 40 International Drum Rudiments.
2. Listen to the recordings mentioned above.
3. Keep your hands relaxed.

"LIFE'S A DRAG" BASIC GROOVE

LIFE'S A DRAG
FILLS UTILIZING DRAGS AND DRAG TAPS

PRACTICE SEGMENTS: COMBINE THE FOLLOWING SEGMENTS TO CREATE FILLS OF YOUR OWN

ld #1

ld #2

ld #3

ld #4

ld #5

ld #6

ld #7

ld #8

ld #9

ld #10

FLAMS ON THE DRAG SHELL

This hybrid rudiment is often referred to as the "Tony Williams lick" (check out "Protocosmos")—but he never overused it. If you listen to an entire Tony Williams record, you won't hear it all that often. Although this may have originated in drumlines and rudimental playing, it eventually found its way into jazz and bebop. If you can play nice, even single drag taps, the next step is to flam the first note. Practice the key segments until they are very smooth. I've written fills using both triplet and sixteenth-note permutations. Depending on your facility and the tempo of the music, these can be very appropriate in various styles. For further discussion, Todd Sucherman does a nice job explaining this on his *Methods and Mechanics* DVD.

Practice Tips

1. Practice the rudiment on the pad first.

2. Keep your hands relaxed.

3. Use a metronome and gradually increase the tempo.

"FLAMS ON THE DRAG SHELL" BASIC GROOVE

STRAIGHT EIGHTHS

WITH SWING FEEL

FLAMS ON THE DRAG SHELL
FILLS WITH FLAMMED DRAG TAPS

PRACTICE SEGMENTS: COMBINE THE FOLLOWING SEGMENTS TO CREATE FILLS OF YOUR OWN

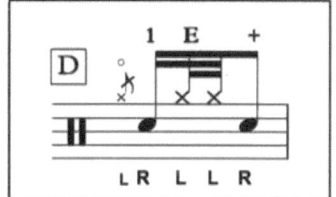

A DIDDLE-DIDDLE

As drummers and percussionists, we really do have a language all to ourselves. Diddles and pataflaflas and flams—its quite lovely and silly. Of course, on this page I'm talking about the paradiddle-diddle, a great rudiment that is so easy to apply to the drumset. You keep your leading hand at the start of each repetition. I call this a circular rudiment, and it has basic swing time built into it. Who knew? This one works great using either sixteenths or triplets. One of my favorite combinations is paradiddle-diddle, paradiddle-diddle, paradiddle. You can hear this rudiment played by many of the jazz masters from early swing to contemporary jazz. Danny Gottlieb, in his book *The Evolution of Jazz Drumming*, mentions that the great Kenny Clarke was using combinations of paradiddle-diddles and paradiddles in his solos!

Practice Tips

1. Practice and memorize the original rudiment on the snare or a practice pad until you are comfortable.

2. Practice the key segments slowly.

3. Notice the dotted quarter-note pulse.

"A DIDDLE-DIDDLE" BASIC GROOVE

A DIDDLE-DIDDLE
FILLS USING PARADIDDLE-DIDDLES

PRACTICE SEGMENTS: COMBINE THE FOLLOWING SEGMENTS TO CREATE FILLS OF YOUR OWN

A DIDDLE-DIDDLE
TWO-BAR PHRASES

PARADIDDLE-DIDDLE 7s

RATAMA WHATS?

Ratamacue? It is not an SAT word, but maybe it should be! This is one of those rudiments that was named after its sound: RA-TA-MA-CUE. There are three versions of this rudiment: single, double, and triple. The only part that changes is how many drags to play: 1, 2 or 3. There was even a song in 1942 entitled "Doin' the Ratamacue" by the Tony Pastor Orchestra. (Watch the video, as you will either laugh or cringe!) Anyway, this is a fun rudiment to orchestrate on the kit. It has been used by many, but most eloquently by Steve Gadd. For a great demonstration, watch the *Hudson Music Master Series: Steve Gadd* DVD. I first learned this rudiment from my drum teacher and from playing the *N.A.R.D.* book. It's fun to utilize this common rudiment around the kit; experiment and have fun with it!

Practice Tips

1. **Practice the single, double, and triple ratamacue.**
2. **Play through the practice segments slowly.**
3. **Gradually increase the tempo.**

"RATAMA WHATS?" BASIC GROOVE

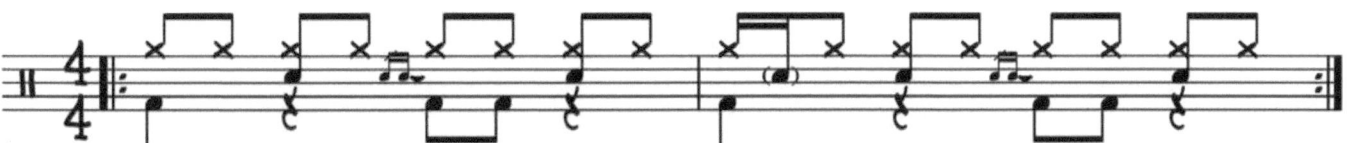

RATAMA WHATS?
FILLS UTILIZING RATAMACUES

PRACTICE SEGMENTS: COMBINE THE FOLLOWING SEGMENTS TO CREATE FILLS OF YOUR OWN

rw #1

248

rw #2

249

rw #3

250

rw #4

251

rw #5

252

rw #6

253

rw #7

254

rw #8

255

rw #9

256

rw #10

257

RUFFIN' THE DRAGS

These fills are really embellishments which have been presented in a new way. As I mentioned earlier, I define a drag as a pair of grace notes executed with a double stroke, and a ruff as a pair of grace notes executed with two single strokes. That said, take a drag that you would normally place before a downbeat with a buzz or double stroke, and split it between both hands. This provides a very interesting sound that has a little swing to it. I use this to give emphasis to a particular beat of the bar. On the following page, I show the original drag and then show my concept for splitting it. I split some on the snare and others on the hi-hat, and some between the snare and hi-hat. This treatment is fun, and it adds a unique sound to the groove. You can hear a nice version of this type of thing on "All Blues" by Los Lobotomys, with both Jeff Porcaro and Vinnie Colaiuta on drums (Vinnie plays the solo).

Practice Tips

1. Check out the recording mentioned above.

2. Play through the practice segments slowly.

3. Use a metronome and gradually increase the tempo.

"RUFFIN' THE DRAGS" BASIC GROOVE

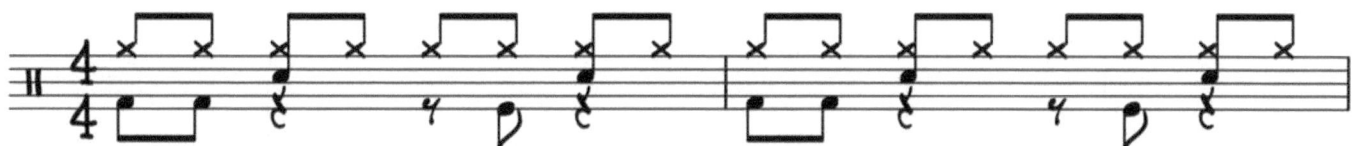

RUFFIN' THE DRAGS
SPLIT THE DRAGS TO R,L RUFF

IMPORTANT: DROP THE LAST EIGHTH NOTE OF THE HI-HAT PART DOWN TO THE HI-HAT FOOT. THIS GIVES THE PART A NICE SNAP, AND MAKES IT FUN TO PLAY

REGULAR DRAGS ON SNARE

SPLIT DRAGS ON SNARE

PUT THE RUFF ON THE HI-HAT

SPLIT THE RUFF BETWEEN THE HI-HAT AND SNARE

ADD A SECOND RUFF BEFORE BEAT 2

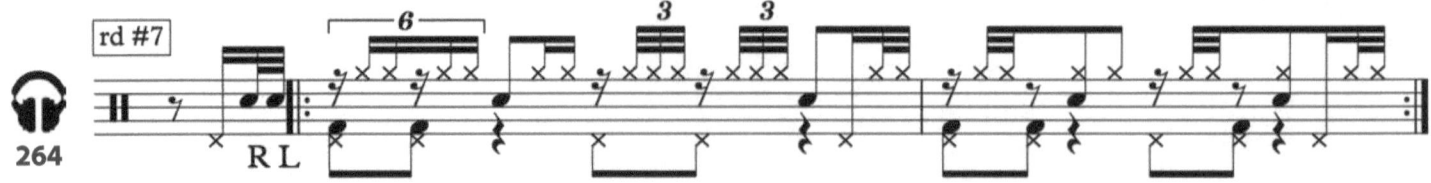

CHAPTER 6
FUNCTIONS

LAYERED FILLS

This page is all about playing open-handed and filling with your natural leading hand, while your non-leading hand holds down the groove! The nice thing about playing open-handed (or "uncrossed") is that you can do things that are almost impossible cross-handed. Check out some of the great open-handed players of our time: Lenny White, Billy Cobham, Carter Beauford, Simon Phillips, Dom Famularo, Will Kennedy, and Claus Hessler, among others. A great recording to study is Carter Beauford on the track "Warehouse" by The Dave Matthews Band.

I feel like the drumming world is moving in this direction little by little. I have most of my students learn to lead both ways. It's proving to be remarkable that many of them play grooves both lefty and righty with equal ease, because they've learned this way from the start. More and more, my playing is going in this direction. Have fun and enjoy the journey!

For further study, check out the books *Open-Handed Playing, Vol. 1* and *Open-Handed Playing, Vol. 2: A Step Beyond* by Claus Hessler.

Practice Tips

1. Check out the artists and recordings mentioned above.
2. Play through the practice segments slowly.
3. Practice playing the fills on one surface while keeping time.
4. Use a metronome and gradually increase the tempo.

"LAYERED FILLS" BASIC GROOVE

Filling In The Grooves/Functions

LAYERED FILLS
PLAYING FILLS WHILE RIDING OPEN-HANDED

PRACTICE SEGMENTS: COMBINE THE FOLLOWING SEGMENTS TO CREATE FILLS OF YOUR OWN

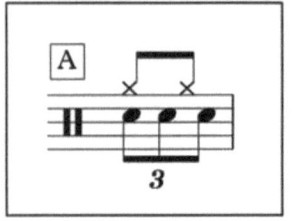
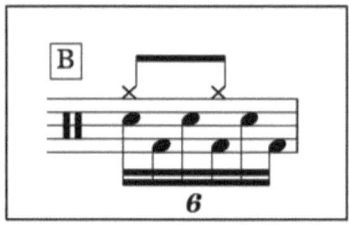
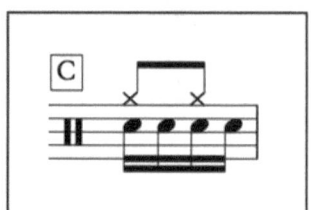
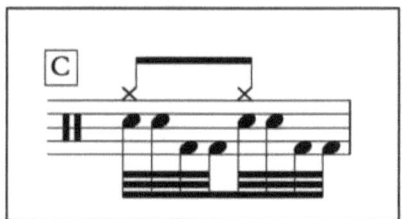

lf #1 — 265

lf #2 — 266
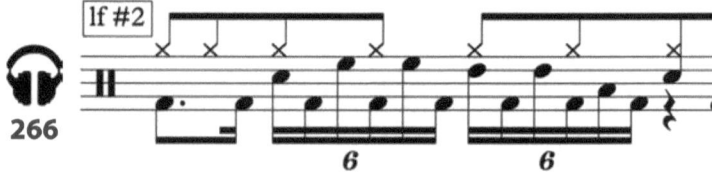

lf #3 — 267

lf #4 — 268

lf #5 — 269
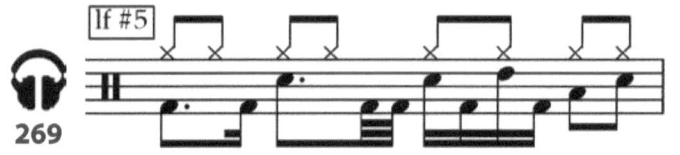

lf #6 — 270

lf #7 — 271
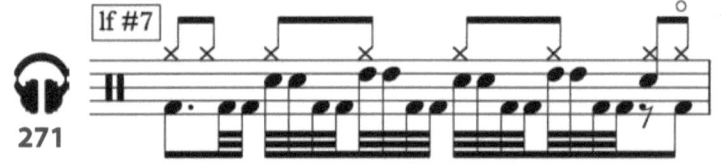

lf #8 — 272
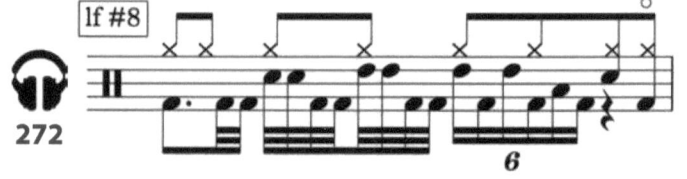

lf #9 — 273

lf #10 — 274

lf #11 — 275
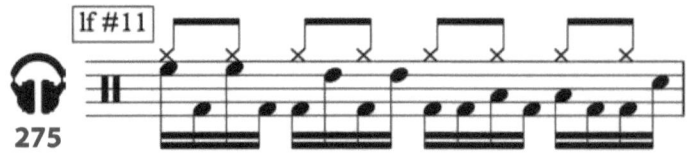

lf #12 — 276

Filling In The Grooves/Functions

SET 'EM UP

This page is all about setting up common figures in music. It is our job to provide a launching pad for the rest of the band when it comes to figures or rhythmic events in the music. We try to make it easy for the rest of the band to hit the figures with confidence, and they should be able to trust that you, the drummer, will deliver the necessary ingredients to make them comfortable. You can hear brilliant ways in which this is done from the likes of Buddy Rich, Roy Haynes, and other jazz and fusion greats that I've mentioned throughout this book!

I have divided this section into two categories, straight and swung, and I tried to include a few different spots for hits and common figures. This page is intended to get you thinking about the space around the hits. This makes it easier to come up with fills that not only set up the hit, but function as a springboard for the band.

Practice Tips

1. Listen to the drummers mentioned above.
2. Count out all of the patterns.
3. Pay close attention to the time and groove.
4. Remember the function of setups.

SETTING UP COMMON FIGURES FOR THE BAND

SET UP THE 2 - SWING (su #1, 277)

SET UP THE 2 - STRAIGHT (su #2, 278)

SET UP THE 3 - SWING (su #3, 279)

SET UP THE 3 - STRAIGHT (su #4, 280)

SET UP THE & OF 2 - SWING (su #5, 281)

SET UP THE & OF 2 - STRAIGHT (su #6, 282)

SET UP THE & OF 4 - SWING (su #7, 283)

SET UP THE & OF 4 - STRAIGHT (su #8, 284)

SET UP THE A OF 4 - SWING (su #9, 285)

SET UP THE A OF 4 - STRAIGHT (su #10, 286)

DISPLACED NOT MISPLACED

Displacement can be a great way to create tension in certain musical settings. Note: I do not recommend using this material in a pop setting. Your singer will fire you before you establish the "one!" This is for music that lends itself to rhythmic exploration (more improvisational music, progressive music, etc.).

The fills that I've written in this context are grooves that have been displaced. The A column shows the original groove, and the B column shows the displacement. Practice playing the A and B for four bars each to become comfortable with the shift. This is a subtle way to play a momentary displacement while keeping the band locked into a familiar sound.

Check out how James Brown drummer, Clyde Stubblefield, was using displacement in his playing as early as 1968 on tracks like "I Got the Feeling." A more contemporary example is "I'm Tweeked," from Vinnie Colaiuta's solo album, which is a really interesting use of displacement. My inspiration for this kind of thing includes Dave Weckl on *Why Not?* with Michel Camilo and all his recordings with Chick Corea's Electrik Band. For an in-depth further study of displacement, check out Gavin Harrison's book *Rhythmic Illusions*.

Practice Tips

1. Listen to the recordings mentioned above.
2. Count out all of the patterns.
3. For each example, play pattern A three times, then play pattern B.
4. Use a metronome and gradually increase the tempo.

Filling In The Grooves/Functions

DISPLACED NOT MISPLACED
FILLS USING DISPLACEMENT

Column "A" Fills: Straight   **Column "B" Fills: Displaced**

dm #1A

287

dm #1B

dm #2A

288

dm #2B

dm #3A

289

dm #3B

dm #4A

290

dm #4B

dm #5A

291

dm #5B

dm #5

292

dm #6

293

THE BIG ENDING

I hear from students all of the time that they are not sure what to play at the ending of a tune, especially when it's a big ending. As a guide, I've provided a simple five-step approach to accomplish this. The big ending is a very individualized thing. Listen to today's top drummers and you will hear a whole bunch of different styles for endings! Check out live footage of your favorite bands or artists. Look back at some legendary shows. Finally, try my steps when you get in the rehearsal room. The most important thing is to be clear and make your choices obvious and use your body movements to convey to the band when you will end. You have to be the musical director when doing this. I usually insert a pause right before a button (i.e., the final note of the song) so the band has time to catch my hit! Check out how Neil Peart sets up the ending for Rush's "Limelight," and how Todd Sucherman ends "Renegade" and "The Grand Illusion" with Styx live.

Play through various styles of grooves and set yourself up to practice a big ending. You should be able to apply this page to rock, shuffles, swing and everything in between.

Practice Tips

1. Check out the recordings mentioned above.

2. Play through the practice segments slowly.

3. Play with intention!

SOME IDEAS FOR ENDING SONGS IN 5 EASY STEPS

1. HOLD THE CHORD - (CYMBAL SWELLS, RUMBLE)
2. THE TRAIL OFF FILL - (RITARD)
3. FIRST STOP
4. EYE CONTACT FOR SET UP
5. BUTTON

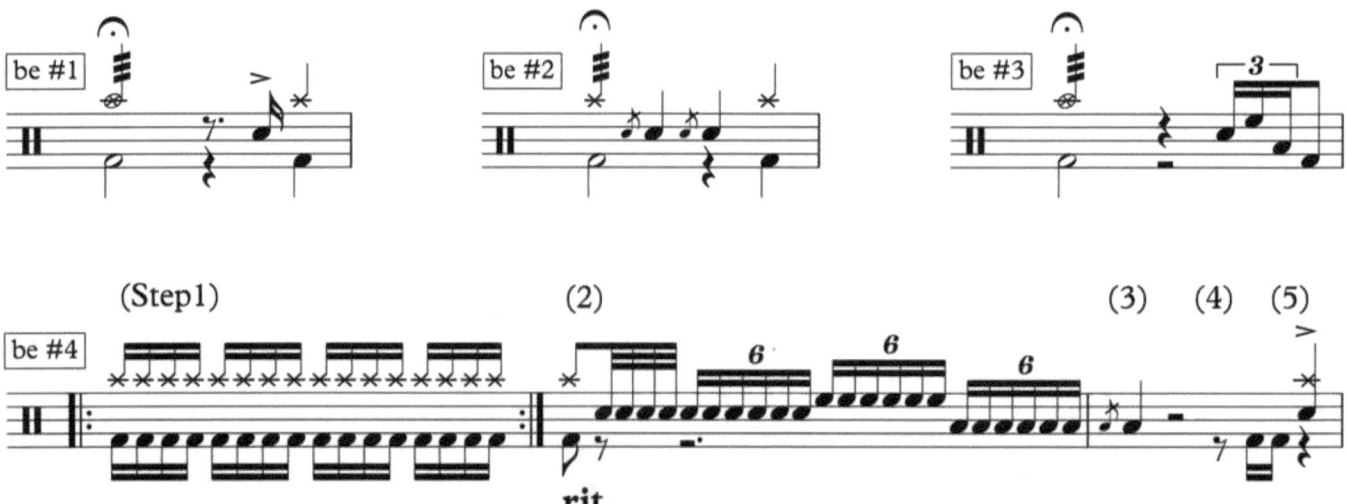

Filling In The Grooves/Functions

Filling In The Grooves/Functions

EXIT STRATEGIES

I always talk about exit strategies with my students when it comes to fills. This concept is about knowing how to come out of a fill and return to the groove cleanly, with conviction and confidence. All too often, I hear students say that they made mistakes coming out of a fill, or they avoid playing certain fills so they don't blow it coming back in, "playing it safe."

Here, using one fill from the "A Diddle-Diddle" page, are some "beat 4 exit strategies." It's vitally important to have a good flow and continuous groove to connect things flawlessly. I like to think of the last quarter note before returning to the groove as the place to do this. Using the same basic fill, we can explore several different exit strategies. The exit strategy can be determined by the tempo and emotion of the song.

Practice Tips

1. Play each fill slowly to gain muscle memory.

2. Use a metronome.

3. Pay close attention to the sticking.

4. Go from groove to fill, and fill back to groove.

"EXIT STRATEGIES" BASIC GROOVE

EXIT STRATEGIES
STRATEGIES FOR RETURNING TO THE GROOVE WHEN EXITING A FILL
ONE FILL, TEN EXIT STRATEGIES

Filling In The Grooves/Footnotes

FOOTNOTES

CHAPTER 7

HOOFS'N'PAWS

This section provides a series of fills that will help you break you away from basic hand-to-hand fills and bring rhythmic interaction with your bass drum foot. If you feel like you're in a rut, playing the same fills over and over, this page can provide a creative launching pad. There are so many possibilities when combining the hands and feet. This approach can be incorporated into any style of music.

I first became interested in developing this type of fill after hearing Ralph Humphrey's fills on "Montana" from Frank Zappa's *Overnite Sensation* album, and then discovering Terry Bozzio on early Zappa recordings as well, in addition to his work on the album *Danger Money* by UK and his *Solo Drums* instructional video. Simon Phillips uses this concept as well, on "Give Blood" by Pete Townsend. I also love Steve Gadd's use of this in his fills and solos.

Try using *Stick Control* by George Lawrence Stone as material for developing dexterity between the hands and feet. For example, play all rights with the hands (alternating strokes) and lefts with the bass drum foot. Then try the opposite approach. For a very simple set of exercises, use lesson 3 from Ted Reed's *Syncopation*. Even though the lesson is written in quarter notes, just use the combinations as movement exercises, and switch to eighth and sixteenth notes as you get more comfortable with each exercise.

Practice Tips

1. **Play each key segment slowly.**
2. **Pay attention to the accents in each fill.**
3. **Play with a metronome!**

"HOOFS'N'PAWS" BASIC GROOVE

HOOFS'N'PAWS
HAND AND FOOT INTERACTION

PRACTICE SEGMENTS: COMBINE THE FOLLOWING SEGMENTS TO CREATE FILLS OF YOUR OWN

MIDDLE FOOT SYNDROME

This page is about a pattern that I first saw on a Dave Weckl video; I then recognized it on the Tony Williams recording "Protocosmos." Mike Portnoy also had a nice idea for this that he credited to Motorhead drummer Mickey Dee. So this lick has been around the block. What I like about it is the melodic change in direction during its execution.

As I mentioned on the "You Be Trippin'" page, it helps to find the shuffle in the pattern. This one has a unique split-shuffle feel: RR-LL. It's like swung double strokes with a kick in between! Got it?

Practice Tips

1. Play with a metronome!

2. Practice the key segments slowly so you feel the middle note.

3. Listen to the shuffle inside the triplet.

"MIDDLE FOOT SYNDROME" BASIC GROOVE

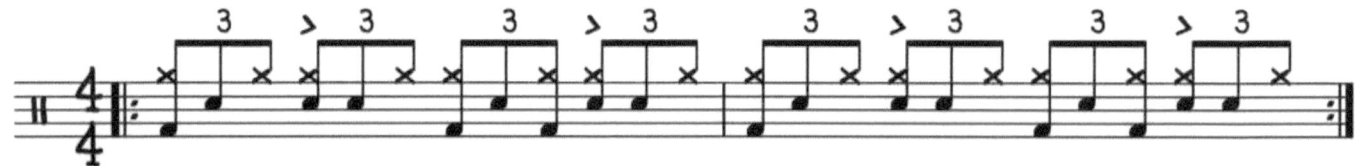

MIDDLE FOOT SYNDROME
THE BASS DRUM ON THE MIDDLE OF THE TRIPLET

PRACTICE SEGMENTS: COMBINE THE FOLLOWING SEGMENTS TO CREATE FILLS OF YOUR OWN

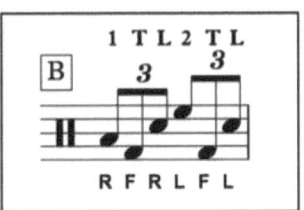

YOU BE TRIPPIN'

This page is about getting your "broken triplets" to not sound broken! I'm talking about da-ka-doo triplets (tom-tom-kick or kick-tom-tom). These are the triplet patterns you hear Steve Gadd play on "Aja" by Steely Dan. Gadd also uses this classic lick on "Tee Bag" from Steps Ahead. John Bonham uses them in his solo on "Moby Dick" and "Stairway to Heaven." You'll also hear this fill used at the ending of every rock song from about 1960 to... well, now! This is a super-common lick, but it needs to be played cleanly, with good separation between the notes. My approach is to find the shuffle in the rhythm—only then can you execute this with the proper accuracy and feel. Once you get the shuffle, the middle note just slips in between.

Practice Tips

1. Play each practice segment slowly.

2. Feel the implied shuffle until it grooves.

3. Practice the fills only after the practice segments are comfortable.

"YOU BE TRIPPIN'" BASIC GROOVE

YOU BE TRIPPIN'

In this section, the practice segments have rests with stickings under the middle note from each eighth-note triplet group, thus creating a shuffle between two limbs. I find that the problem most students have with this type of triplet fill is attaining the clarity needed to make the fill sound great. If you feel the shuffle in each sticking, this fill will groove hard. Find the shuffle, and practice slowly!

PRACTICE SEGMENTS: COMBINE THE FOLLOWING SEGMENTS TO CREATE FILLS OF YOUR OWN

THUNDER FROM DOWN UNDER

Double bass fills are a way to make a big statement. I've always had a love for double bass drumming. In my formative years I learned how to organize my approach to double bass with Joe Franco's book *Double Bass Drumming*, which was the first book to provide a system for learning this skill. Later on I wrote my own book, *Double Bass Boot Camp*. Also, check out *Pedal Control* by Dom Famularo and Joe Bergamini with Stephane Chamberland.

The history of double bass drum kits goes back to 1939, when Louie Bellson sketched a double bass kit for his art project in school. Then in 1946, Bellson did his first gig with a double bass setup. In later years it grew in popularity with such talent as Billy Cobham, Keith Moon, Ginger Baker, Cozy Powell, Tommy Aldridge, Carmine Appice, and Neil Peart. Some great recorded examples of double bass go back to Carmine Appice on Vanilla Fudge's "Shotgun," Billy Cobham's double bass shuffle "Quadrant 4," and Simon Phillips' odd-meter double bass shuffle on Jeff Beck's "Space Boogie." Also check out Terry Bozzio on Frank Zappa's *Live in New York* album and his work on *Heavy Metal Bebop* with the Brecker Brothers. These days Virgil Donati, Simon Phillips, and Thomas Lang are a few prominent double bass players in the progressive and fusion genres. Then, of course, there's the metal genre with all of its sub-genres, providing a wealth of material with breakneck speed and technical prowess. Gene Hoglan of Testament, Derek Roddy from Serpents Rise, and Tomas Haake from Meshuggah, to name a few, have an amazing body of work with killer double bass. This page is dedicated to all of those drummers, and provides a simple guide to some fun and interesting double bass drum fills..

Practice Tips

1. Listen to recordings using double bass grooves and fills.

2. Sit up straight and stay relaxed.

3. Use a metronome and always count.

"THUNDER FROM DOWN UNDER" BASIC GROOVE

THUNDER FROM DOWN UNDER
DOUBLE BASS/DOUBLE PEDAL FILLS

PRACTICE SEGMENTS: COMBINE THE FOLLOWING SEGMENTS TO CREATE FILLS OF YOUR OWN

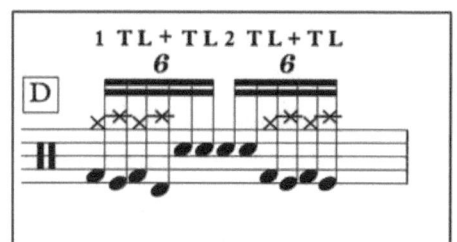

du #1

du #2

du #3

du #4

332

du #5

333

du #6

du #7

334

du #8

335

du #9

336

du #10

337

LOOK MOM, NO HANDS
(Fills with Just the Feet)

These fills are so fun—and usually unexpected. When I employ one of these fills, it often gets a great reaction from the band as well as the audience. There is such a sonic change that occurs when you drop it all down to the kick drum. These fills are especially effective when there is a space in the music. Great examples of this are in Simon Phillips' performance on "Give Blood," by Pete Townshend, and Dave Weckl's playing on "Just Kidding" from Michel Camilo's album *Why Not?* I also love Steve Gadd's use of this concept in his solos; when I first heard him play an idea like this, I thought, "Wow, that's different!" Just a bar of eighth notes can have an impact to the dynamics range of a song; fills don't have to be complicated in order to be effective! A couple other listening examples are Vinnie Colaiuta on "Keep it Greasey" by Frank Zappa and Simon Phillips on "Big Neighborhood" by Lee Ritenour.

I think you'll find these fills to be great fun!

Practice Tips

1. Work on each fill slowly, with control.

2. Sit up straight, as balance may be an issue at first.

3. Use a metronome and gradually increase the tempo.

"LOOK MOM, NO HANDS" BASIC GROOVE

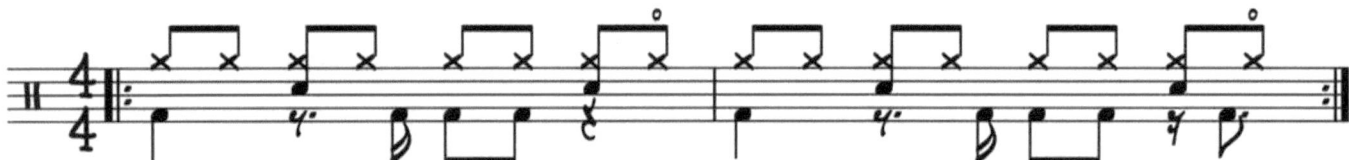

LOOK MOM, NO HANDS
FILLING WITH THE FEET

PRACTICE SEGMENTS: COMBINE THE FOLLOWING SEGMENTS TO CREATE FILLS OF YOUR OWN

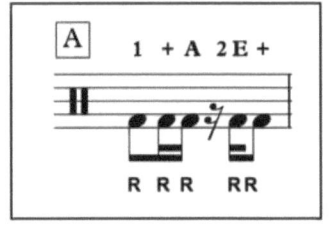
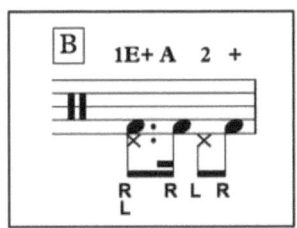

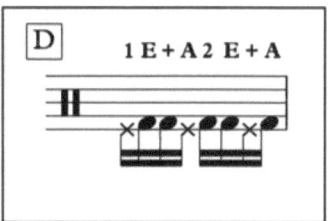

nh #1

338

nh #2

339

nh #3

340

nh #4

341

nh #5

342

nh #6

343

nh #7
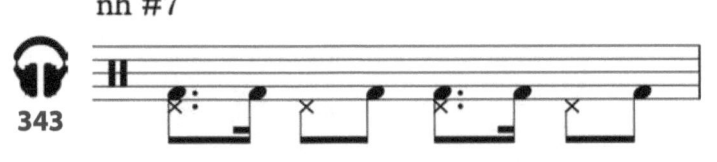
343

nh #8
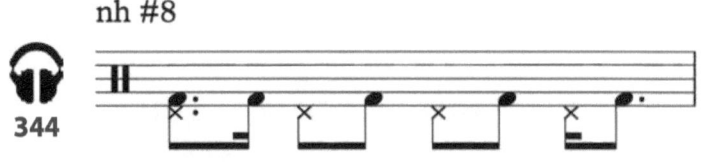
344

nh #9
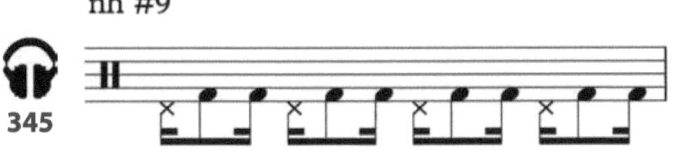
345

nh #10
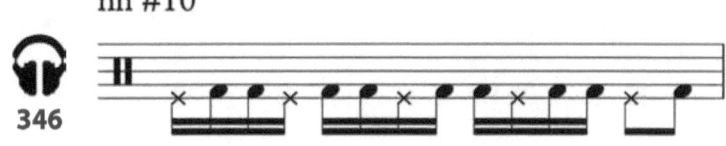
346

87

HAND ME DOWNS

This page is not only comprised of fills, but acts as a series of exercises to help you gain better facility at fills that start with the feet and end with the hands (or vice versa). They can be played as one-bar phrases or combined to create new phrases. For simplicity's sake, they are played between the feet and the hands on the snare drum. Feel free to move these around the drumset.

My inspiration for this page starts with Louie Bellson and his solo on "Skin Deep" (Duke Ellington) from 1957. I later discovered Terry Bozzio, Rod Morgenstein and other double bass and double-pedal players such as Mike Portnoy and Virgil Donati.

Practice Tips

1. Play each exercise slowly, with a metronome.
2. Move from one exercise to another smoothly.
3. Count each exercise out loud.
4. Try each fill in time with a groove.

"HAND ME DOWNS" BASIC GROOVE

HAND ME DOWNS

"Hand me downs" refer to sixteenth-note triplets that are split between the hands and feet. These segments work very well as stand-alone fills or in conjunction with other ideas.

LATINISH

This page has a group of fills that I play during Latin feels. I don't claim to be the authority on Latin jazz by any means, but I know what feels good, and I enjoy this music very much! Over the years, many drummers in this area have inspired me. Early on, I saw Robby Ameen playing in New York with Dave Valentin, and then bought his album *Live at the Blue Note*. I love all of Chick Corea's Latin-infused jazz. I was particularly inspired by Dave Weckl's playing on Michel Camilo's record *Why Not*, Joel Rosenblatt's playing on Camilo's self-titled album, and Paquito D'Rivera's *Why Not*, with Porthino and Dave Weckl on drums. Lately I've been listening to Dafnis Prieto's album *About the Monks*, Horacio Hernandez with Gonzalo Rubalcaba, and Ignacio Berroa on his record *Codes*.

For further study, check out Horacio Hernandez's book *Conversations in Clave*, Ignacio Berroa's book *Groovin' in Clave*, and Berroa's *Mastering Afro-Cuban Drumming* DVD. For an introduction to playing Afro-Cuban rhythms with a stylistically correct approach, the book *Afro-Cuban Rhythms for Drumset*, by Frank Malabe and Bob Weiner, is a classic.

Practice Tips

1. Listen to the recordings mentioned above.
2. Play through the practice segments slowly.
3. Use a metronome and gradually increase the tempo.
4. Pay attention to clave at all times.

"LATINISH" BASIC GROOVES

Filling In The Grooves/Styles

LATINISH
FILLS INFUENCED BY LATIN JAZZ AND FUSION

lh #1

359

lh #2

360

lh #3

361

lh #4

362

lh #5

363

lh #6

364

lh #7

365

lh #8

lh #9

365

lh #10

366

DROP ONE IN

Even if you don't have many opportunities to play traditional reggae, you'll find reggae grooves and their derivatives, like the "one-drop," throughout pop and rock music. The one-drop groove gets its nickname from the single bass drum note on beat 3 of the bar.

This groove was made popular by Bob Marley and the Wailers, with Carlton Barrett on drums. "Get Up Stand Up," "One Love," and many other classic Bob Marley tunes have this groove. Also check out "Lucille" by Frank Zappa and "Solid Love" by Joni Mitchell, both with Vinnie Colaiuta putting his spin on the one-drop groove. The Police were heavily influenced by reggae, demonstrated on tracks like "Walking on the Moon," "Every Little Thing She Does is Magic," and many others. Stewart Copeland does some wonderfully tasteful playing on these tracks.

If you get to play a classic one-drop groove, you have to keep it tasteful and grooving hard, without losing the one-drop (beat 3) during the fill! I like to plant the fill around the kick note in the middle of the bar, as this keeps the forward momentum of the groove. You don't want to emphasize the 1, but rather the 4 or the "and" of 4 at the end of these fills.

Practice Tips

1. Listen to the recordings mentioned above.
2. Count out all of the patterns.
3. Keep the one-drop within the fills.
4. Don't rush!

"DROP ONE IN" BASIC GROOVE

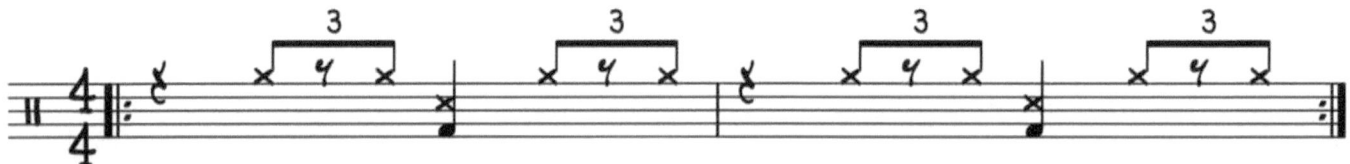

DROP ONE IN
ONE DROP REGGAE FILLS

NAWLINS STYLE

The fills on this page are influenced by New Orleans-style funk and R&B. I've been influenced by the great drummers and music from New Orleans, starting with Zigaboo Modeliste, the godfather of New Orleans funk and groove. Check out Zigaboo on "Cissy Strut" and "Hey Pocky A-Way" by The Meters. I love the Neville Brothers' "Fire on The Bayou," Professor Longhair's "Big Chief" and "Jambalaya," and Dr. John's "Right Way." Other recordings to check out include James Black's playing on "The Hook and Sling" by Eddie Bo, The Dirty Dozen Brass Band's "Inside Straight" and "Kid Jordan's Second Line," and Johnny Vidacovich on Professor Longhair's "Crawfish Fiesta." "Cat and Mouse" by Vital Information, with Steve Smith on drums, has a fusion slant on the New Orleans style.

There is a New Orleans Second Line element to much of this content. Remember, these fills are influenced by this style. If you want to study the style more closely, make sure you check out traditional New Orleans drumming. In addition to listening to the music, a great resource is Stanton Moore's book *Groove Alchemy*.

At the end of this section there is a simple play-along track to get your feet wet and put the fills to use!

Practice Tips

1. Listen to many recordings in this style.
2. Play this section with a slight swing.
3. Think of the 3/2 clave.

"NAWLINS STYLE" BASIC GROOVE

NAWLINS STYLE
FILLS INFLUNCED BY NEW ORLEANS-STYLE DRUMMING

PRACTICE SEGMENTS: COMBINE THE FOLLOWING SEGMENTS TO CREATE FILLS OF YOUR OWN

387
with click

388
no click

NAWLINS STYLE

♩ = 100

TOSCANO, GREEN, VALDES

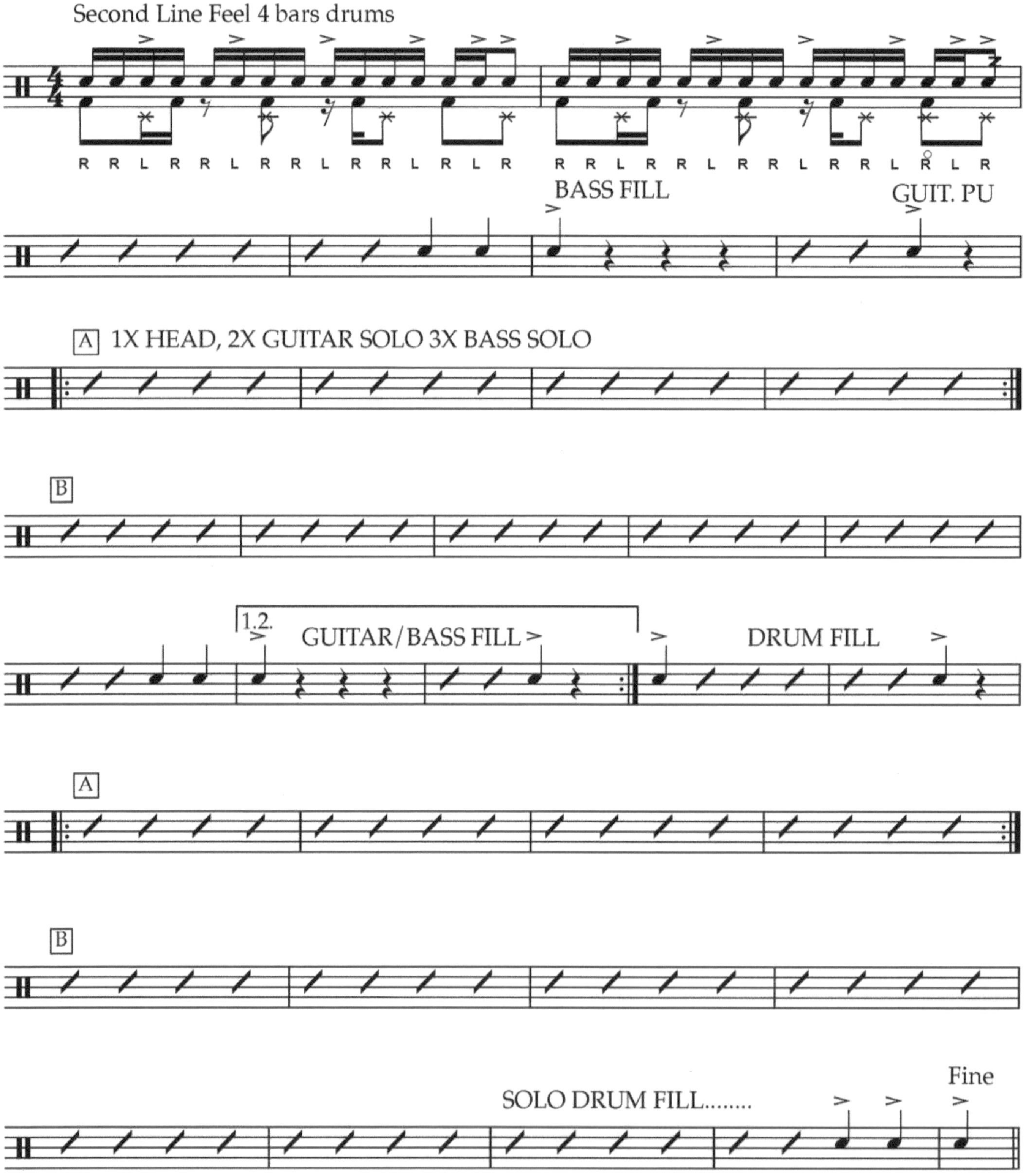

Filling In The Grooves/Styles

GOT THE BLUES?

This group of fills is all about straight-ahead slow to medium-tempo blues. Think of Stevie Ray Vaughan's "Texas Flood," Buddy Miles' "Texas," and B.B. King's "Key to the Highway." Some prominent blues players are S.P. Leary, Sam Lay, and one of my favorites, Jim Keltner. Outside of traditional blues, check out "Goodbye Pork Pie Hat" by Jeff Beck, with Richard Bailey on drums, and "The Torture Never Stops" by Frank Zappa, with Terry Bozzio on drums.

Having a solid group of fills in your back pocket will give you confidence and help you relax, so you can take care of the task at hand: playing solid time! You don't want to feel stuck playing the same couple of fills all the time. The ideas on this page will hopefully give you a new palette from which to choose and create some of your own ideas. Simplicity is the key to success in this area, but simple doesn't have to be boring!

Practice Tips

1. Listen to the recordings mentioned above and others in this style.

2. Do not rush!

3. Play these examples with time over eight-, twelve-, and sixteen-bar cycles.

BASIC SLOW BLUES GROOVE

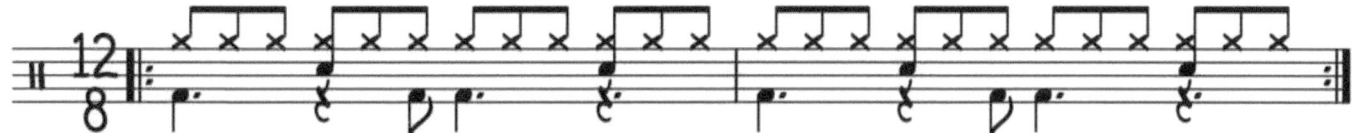

Filling In The Grooves/Styles

GOT THE BLUES?
BLUES-INSPIRED FILLS, SLOW TO MEDIUM TEMPO

PRACTICE SEGMENTS: COMBINE THE FOLLOWING SEGMENTS TO CREATE FILLS OF YOUR OWN

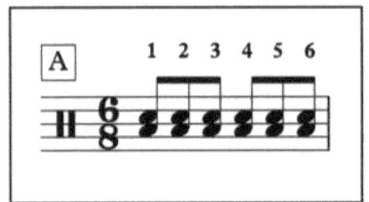

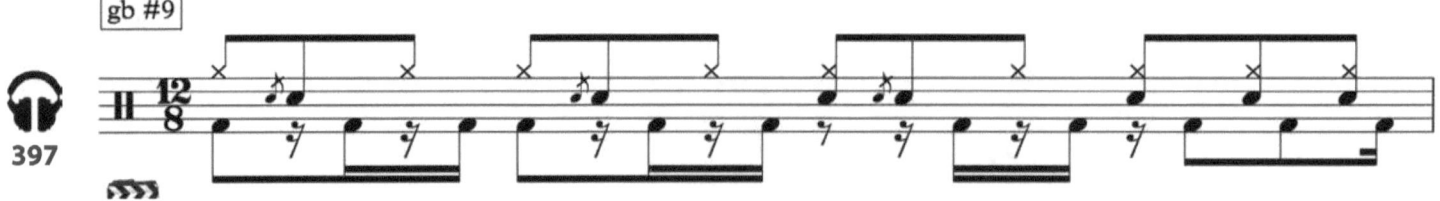

Filling In The Grooves/Styles

GOT THE BLUES

399
with click

400
no click

Toscano, Greene, Valdes

♩. = 56

SHUFFLING ALONG

Playing a good shuffle is a must for any drummer. Knowing how to fill in this context, while keeping great time and making it feel right, is imperative! I love all kinds of shuffles, from jazz to funk and rock. Check out Jeff Porcaro on Steely Dan's "Black Friday" and "Lido Shuffle," Chris Layton on Stevie Ray Vaughan's "Pride and Joy," Omar Hakim on Sting's "Shadows in the Rain," and Jim Gordon on "Caledonia" by B.B. King.

There are many different shuffle feels, but this page is all about the basic blues shuffle. Every artist that I work with uses shuffles in their music, so you need to be comfortable with this feel. Over time, I've developed a pretty large bank of fills to call upon in this style, and this section provides a few nice ideas that work well with different types of shuffles.

For further study, play along to the shuffle tracks in the books *Groove Essentials* by Tommy Igoe and *Survival Guide for the Modern Drummer* by Jim Riley.

Practice Tips

1. Listen to recordings in this style.
2. Play with a relaxed feel.
3. Use a metronome and gradually increase the tempo.

BASIC SLOW BLUES GROOVE

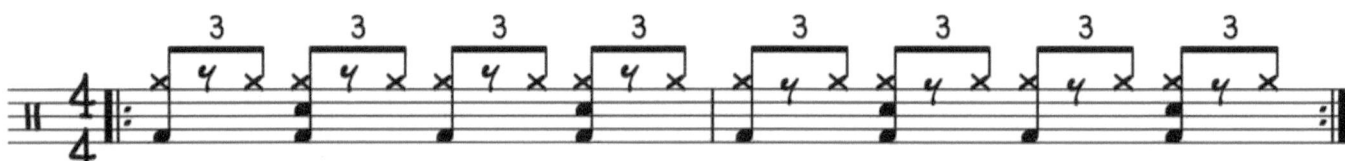

SHUFFLING ALONG
FILLS THAT COMPLIMENT SHUFFLES

PRACTICE SEGMENTS: COMBINE THE FOLLOWING SEGMENTS TO CREATE FILLS OF YOUR OWN

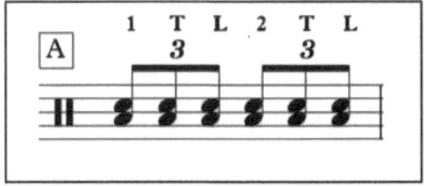

sa #1
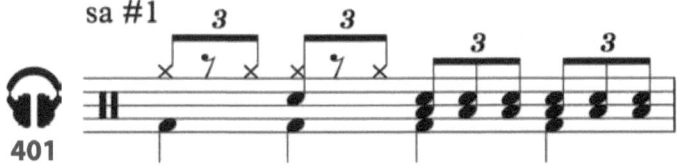
401

sa #2
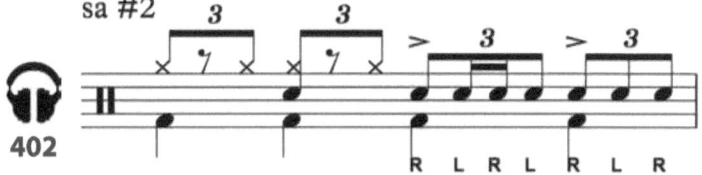
402

sa #3

403

sa #4

404

sa #5

405

sa #6
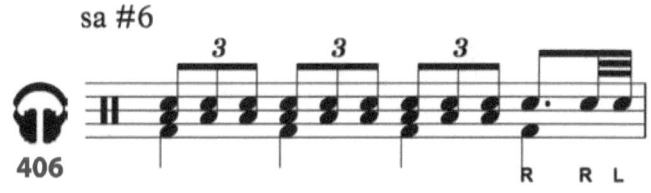
406

sa #7

407

sa #8

408

sa #9

409

sa #10
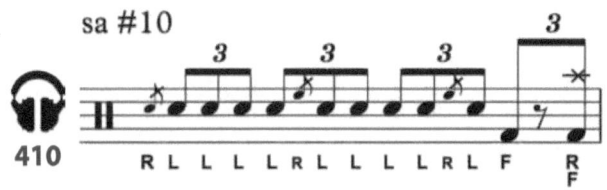
410

Filling In The Grooves/Styles

411
with click

412
no click

SHUFFLING ALONG

TOSCANO, GREENE, VALDES

♩ = 123

Filling In The Grooves/Styles

GET ON THE TRAIN

"Simple yet effective" is the theme of this page. The train beat has a long history in roots and Americana music, most prominently in country and bluegrass. I first heard this beat in the song "The Devil Went Down to Georgia," by the Charlie Daniels Band with James W. Marshall on drums. A couple other classic train beat songs are "Cocaine Blues" by Hank Williams III and "Orange Blossom Special" by Johnny Cash. I never knew I would have to play this feel so often, but I use it all the time with artists that I work with.

The train beat is something that sounds very simple, but can cause problems if not played relaxed and with the correct emphasis. The leading hand plays the backbeat. Using the Moeller method with a combination of upstrokes and downstrokes will accomplish this very well. The non-leading hand plays tap strokes and various accent patterns. I use this beat more often now than ever, playing classic country and working with songwriters in the roots genres. These fills are functional, not groundbreaking! For further study on this feel, check out Jim Riley's book *Survival Guide for the Modern Drummer*.

Practice Tips

1. Listen to the recordings mentioned above.

2. Practice eighth notes using low Moeller strokes in your leading hand.

3. Keep your hand relaxed.

4. Use a metronome and gradually increase the tempo.

BASIC TRAIN BEAT

GET ON THE TRAIN
FILLS THAT COMPLIMENT TRAIN BEATS

PRACTICE SEGMENTS: COMBINE THE FOLLOWING SEGMENTS TO CREATE FILLS OF YOUR OWN

gt #1

413

gt #2

414

gt #3

415

gt #4

416

gt #5
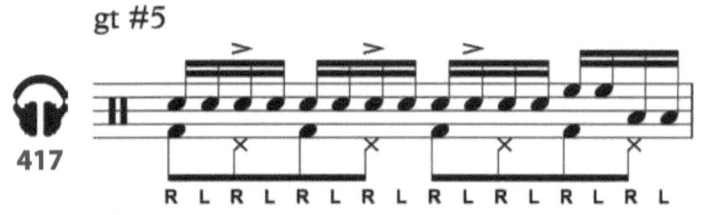
417

gt #6
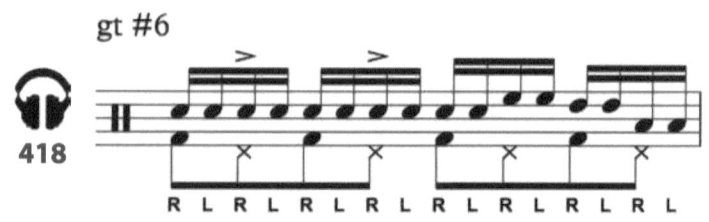
418

gt #7

419

gt #8

420

gt #9
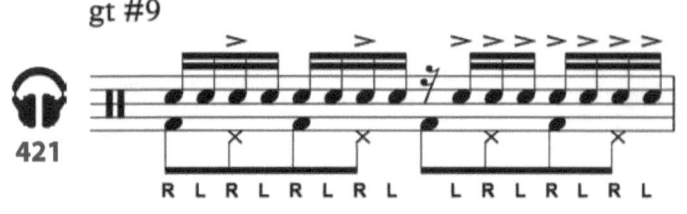
421

gt #10
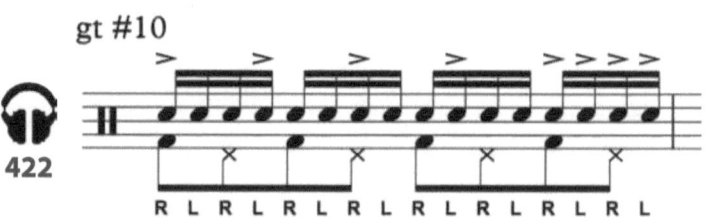
422

423
with click

424
no click

GET ON THE TRAIN

♩ = 127
Brushes
Guitar pick-up

TOSCANO, GREENE, VALDES

Filling In The Grooves/Styles

SWINCOPATION

This section is based on filling in the cracks with syncopated figures. I first learned this concept studying with Kim Plainfield and later with Marvin "Smitty" Smith. This is not a new concept, as you can hear these phrases on countless jazz records, and it is very effective. Alan Dawson pioneered some great applications in this format. Check out Steve Gadd on "Tee Bag" by Steps Ahead and Vinnie Colaiuta on "Slink" (from his self-titled solo album) to hear examples of this concept. The idea is to play a syncopated figure on the ride cymbal and bass drum, and fill in the cracks on the snare drum. A great resource for this section is using exercises from Ted Reed's *Syncopation*. Just do a little swing conversion on the eighths and quarters. Utilize my practice segments and you will be on your way!

For further study check out the book *Advanced Concepts* by Kim Plainfield.

Practice Tips

1. Listen to recordings in this style.
2. Play with a relaxed feel.
3. Keep 2 and 4 on the hi-hat foot.

"SWINCOPATION" BASIC GROOVE

106

SWINCOPATION
A SYSTEM FOR SYNCOPATED FIGURES

PRACTICE SEGMENTS: COMBINE THE FOLLOWING SEGMENTS TO CREATE FILLS OF YOUR OWN

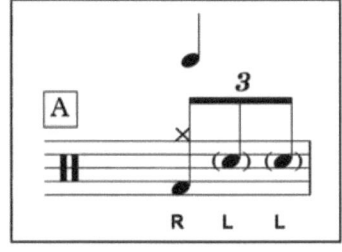
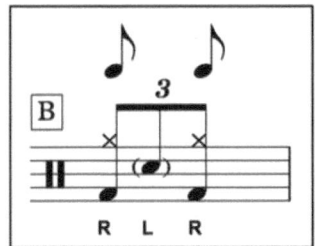
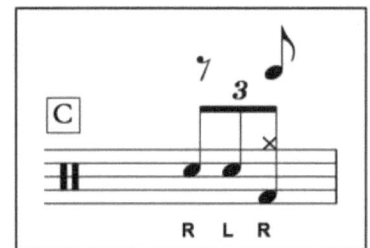
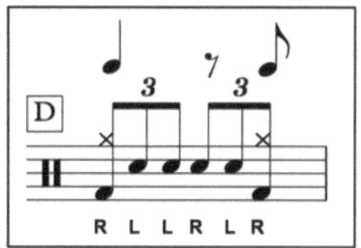

NOT YOUR GRANDMA'S WALTZ

For some drummers, playing in 3/4 is out of their comfort zone, and fill choices are not that obvious. When people think of a waltz, they often think of Strauss or Brahms. Some immediately think of the jazz waltzes, like "All Blues," by Miles Davis, or "Waltz for Debby," by Bill Evans, which are great compositions. But the waltz is also more common than you think in contemporary pop and rock music as well. Think of Mitch Mitchell on "Manic Depression" by Jimi Hendrix, Liberty DeVitto on "Piano Man" by Billy Joel, and Chad Smith on "Breaking the Girl" by the Red Hot Chili Peppers. Another, more subtle track is "Up from Your Life" by James Taylor, with Carlos Vega on drums.

This page presents a sampling of fills in three. I play in musical situations where three is very common, so I wanted to share some of my ideas.

Practice Tips

1. Set a metronome to 3/4 time.
2. Practice playing a simple 3/4 groove.
3. Play through each example while counting out loud.

BASIC ROCK WALTZ

NOT YOUR GRANDMA'S WALTZ
FILLS FOR A MODERN OR ROCK WALTZ

PRACTICE SEGMENTS: COMBINE THE FOLLOWING SEGMENTS TO CREATE FILLS OF YOUR OWN

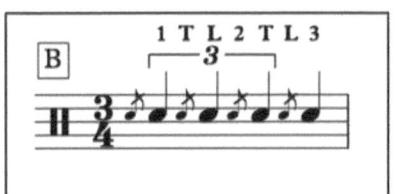

NOT YOUR GRANDMA'S WALTZ

(RIVER RUNS DRY - GIANT FLYING TURTLES)

443

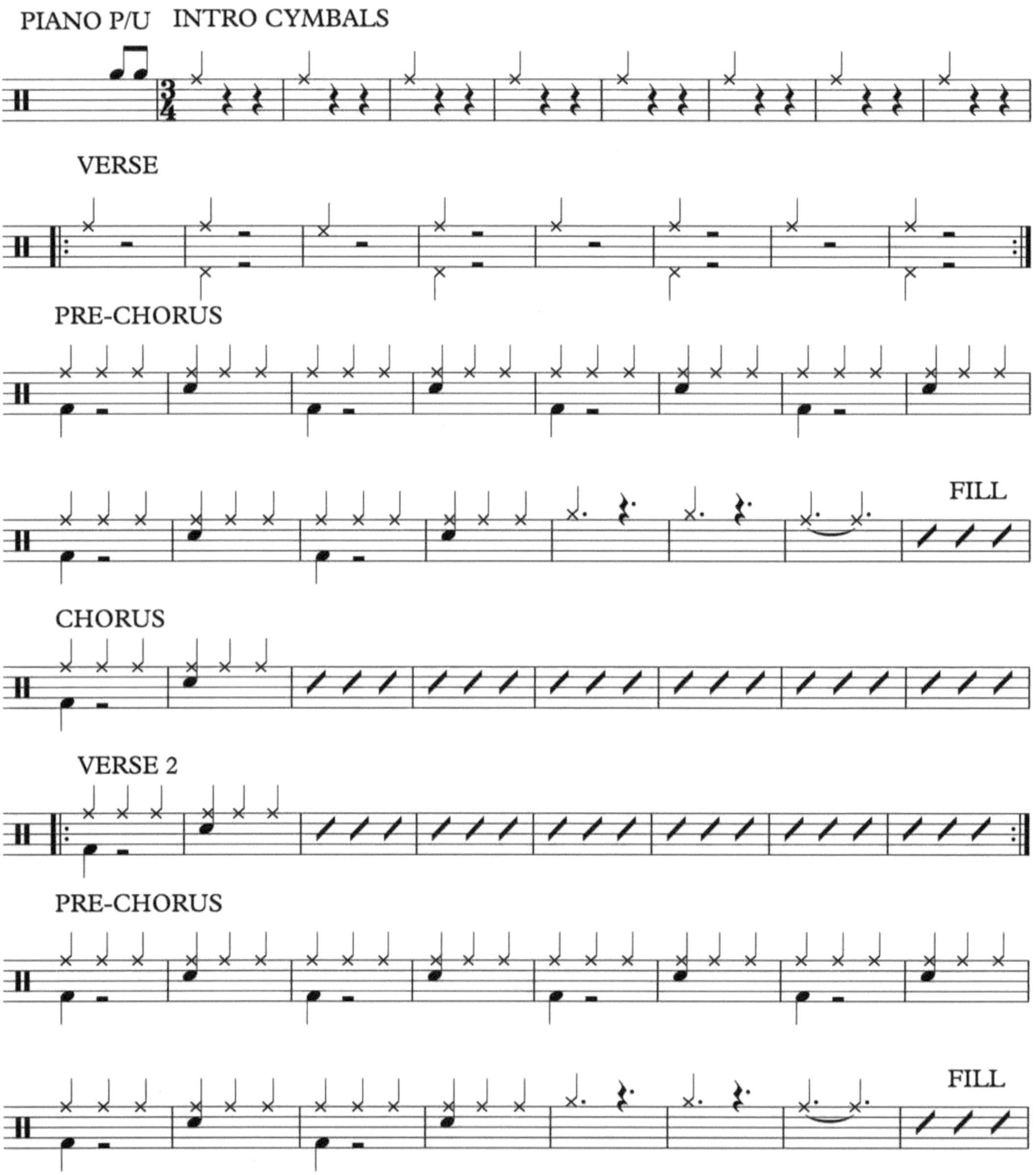

Filling In The Grooves/Styles

SIX OR ONE HALF DOZEN

This is one of my favorite areas of music. Playing in 6/8 time is one of my strong suits and I am fortunate to play music in this time signature often. I enjoy the sound of Afro-Cuban 6/8 music with roots from Niger and Benin. American music in 6/8 always gets my attention as well. There's a lot of room for interpretation in 6/8. It can be "interchanged" with 3/4 time, which allows for some interesting freedom. There are tons of pop and rock songs in 6/8, like "Norwegian Wood" by the Beatles, "Iris" by The Goo Goo Dolls, "Kiss from a Rose" by Seal, and "The Kill" by 30 Seconds to Mars.

You will also want to go back to the roots and study 6/8 in jazz and fusion. For a great place to start, check out "Cachao's Guiro" by Cachao or "Afro-Blue" by Mongo Santamaria. For some fusion in 6/8, listen to "Song to the Pharoah Kings" by Return to Forever (Lenny White on drums), "P.O.V." from Simon Phillips' album *Another Lifetime*, and "Titan" from Bill Connors, with Dave Weckl on drums. The play-along in this section provides a relaxed feel with a couple of twists and turns. Enjoy!

Practice Tips

1. Listen to the recordings mentioned above.
2. Feel the implied "two" feel.
3. Practice counting 6/8 and 3/4 time interchangeably.
4. Use a metronome and gradually increase the tempo.

BASIC 6/8 GROOVE

SIX OR ONE HALF DOZEN
FILLS IN 6/8 TIME

PRACTICE SEGMENTS: COMBINE THE FOLLOWING SEGMENTS TO CREATE FILLS OF YOUR OWN

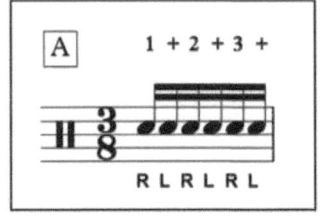
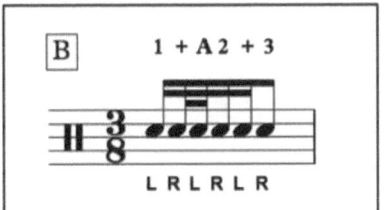
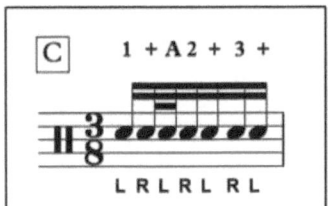

SIX OR ONE HALF DOZEN

454

Toscano, Ferrara

♩. = 67

HATWORK

CHAPTER 9

YOUR BARK IS WORSE THAN YOUR BITE

Barks are short hi-hat openings, typically a sixteenth or an eighth note long, that are punched as accents. The following fills incorporate this technique. There are many influences for this material, starting with funk and fusion. A well-placed, clean bark can feel great and be super funky. Among my earliest influences for hi-hat barks are two Jeff Beck tracks: "Led Boots," with Narada Michael Walden on drums, and "Thelonius," with Richard Bailey on drums—both killer tracks. Led Zeppelin's "Royal Orleans" highlights some great work by John Bonham in this area.

Practice Tips

1. Make sure you pay attention to where the hi-hat closes.
2. Make sure the hi-hat openings and closings are in time.
3. Use a metronome and gradually increase the tempo.
4. Use the shoulder of the stick on the hi-hat for a thicker sound.

"YOUR BARK..." BASIC GROOVE

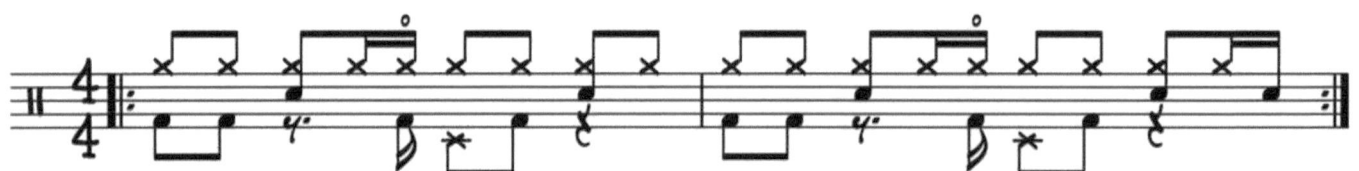

YOUR BARK IS WORSE THAN YOUR BITE
FILLS USING HI-HAT BARKS

PRACTICE SEGMENTS: COMBINE THE FOLLOWING SEGMENTS TO CREATE FILLS OF YOUR OWN

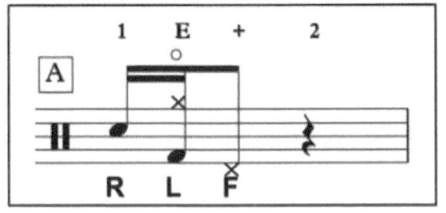

bw #1

455

bw #2

456

bw #3

457

bw #4

458

bw #5

459

bw #6

460

bw #7

461

bw #8

462

bw #9

463

bw #10

464

AND FOR MY NEXT TRICK, I WILL PULL A FILL OUT OF MY HAT

These fills can be magical. The idea of the hi-hat being an important voice on the drumset goes back to pre-bop drummers. In contemporary drumming, Stewart Copeland has become synonymous with the hi-hat, and rightly so: he is prolific on that voice of the drum kit. In funk and groove playing, the hi-hat as a voice for fills seems natural.

The other point to make about hi-hat fills is that while they provide a nice color and make a nice canvas for fills, you can keep the backbeat grooving while you dance around it with the fill. Check out "Driven to Tears" by The Police (Stewart Copeland on drums), "Hello and Goodbye" by Michel Camilo (Dave Weckl on drums), and "Jigsaw" by Mike Stern (Dennis Chambers on drums).

Practice Tips

1. Listen to artists known for their hi-hat work, like the ones mentioned above.

2. Count out all of the patterns.

3. Play these examples on one surface to get familiar with the pattern.

4. Use a metronome and gradually increase the tempo.

"HI-HAT FILLS" BASIC GROOVE

AND FOR MY NEXT TRICK, I WILL PULL A FILL OUT OF MY HAT
FILLS FEATURING THE HI-HAT

PRACTICE SEGMENTS: COMBINE THE FOLLOWING SEGMENTS TO CREATE FILLS OF YOUR OWN

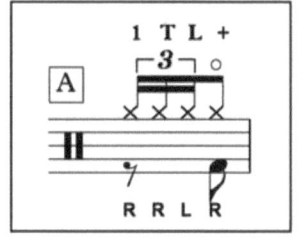
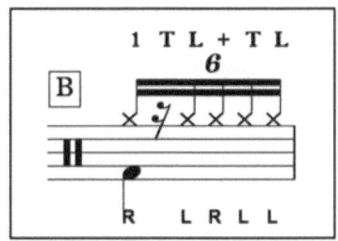
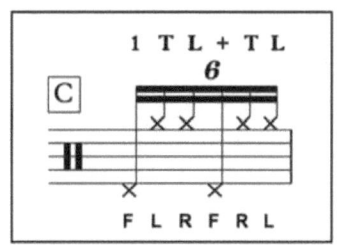
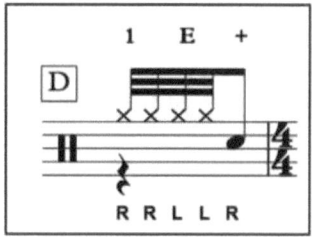

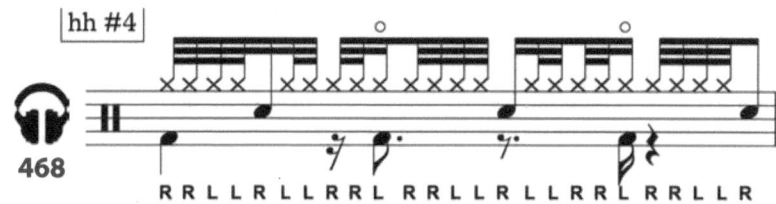

FILLING IN THE GROOVE

The title of this book (and this page) is about playing fills that groove. Some drummers treat drum fills as separate parts of the music, forgetting that *it's all about the groove*—and the fills have to match the energy and emotion of the song they are complementing. These fills are meant to feel like grooves when they stand alone. Groove-fills are meant to embellish the groove without actually taking a detour around the drumset. Once again I refer to David Garibaldi with Tower of Power for brilliant work in this area. Clyde Stubblefield, John "Jabo" Starks and Zigaboo Modeliste all had a way of providing a small variation in the groove to serve the song, much in the way a drum fill would! Listen to Dave Weckl on "Just Kidding" by Michel Camilo for a different type of groove-fills.

Practice Tips

1. Listen to the drummers mentioned above.

2. Count out all of the patterns.

3. Start slowly and play the fills with the groove in mind.

4. Use a metronome and gradually increase the tempo.

"FILLING IN THE GROOVE" BASIC GROOVE

FILLING IN THE GROOVE
FILLS WITHIN A GROOVE

PRACTICE SEGMENTS: COMBINE THE FOLLOWING SEGMENTS TO CREATE FILLS OF YOUR OWN

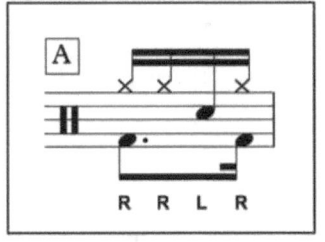

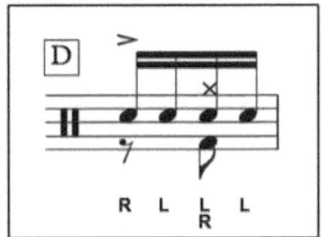

EXTRAS
PLAY-ALONG TRACKS

CHAPTER 10

ONE OF A KIND

This track is from Giant Flying Turtles, a New York City band that I play and record with. To me the tune feels like a classic progressive rock tune with a pop chorus. I've included an instrumental mix to create space for musical creativity.

The song has a main theme which has a triplet feel at 120 BPM. The verses and guitar solo are more of a straight rock feel at 90 BPM. The chorus is a driving eighth-note feel on the toms, also at 90 BPM. Use fills from the book to connect sections and provide momentum. I suggest using "Hoofs and Paws," "Two Hands are Better than One," and "Go Figure."

Use your creativity and have fun!

WALTZ TO THE WORLD

This is another track from the Giant Flying Turtles self-titled debut album. The song has a very loose feel at times, with lots of space for toms and cymbals. It then goes into a straight pop/rock chorus. The form is a little strange, with a 10-bar intro. The verse is 15 bars long, with a 2-bar build into the chorus. The chorus is 7 bars long as it returns to the intro. I would use fills from "Less is More." Toward the end of the song I use ideas from "A Diddle-Diddle." Take advantage of the space in the intro and bridge to play tasteful fills that bring us to the simple verses.

PUFFS OF SMOKE

This track is from artist Roger Street Friedman, with whom I've played for years. This is from his second release, *Shoot the Moon*. It's a bluesy rock track with great horn parts and an interesting form.

This one provides plenty of space for setup fills and even feature fills at the end of the song. It's a great example of being a team player while having some nice spots to bring your own flare!

Enjoy this track and happy drumming!

SHOOT THE MOON

This track is from artist Roger Street Friedman and is the title cut from his second release, *Shoot the Moon*. It's a swingy rock track with a relaxed feel. It has a slight reggae feel in the bridge and some cool phrasing that keeps you on your toes. Check out the fun fiddle solo before the last verse. The little jam at the end is followed by a sharp horn figure that I came up with to wrap up the song. You can draw from many of the fills in this book to compliment the song!

Enjoy this track and happy drumming!

Filling In The Grooves/Extras

486

WALTZ TO THE WORLD

♩ = 110.7

GIANT FLYING TURTLES

INTRO - RIDE LOOSE

FILL

VERSE 1-HI-HAT REPEAT 7X   2-BAR BUILD

CHORUS ROCK

FILL

RIDE LOOSE   FILL   FILL   FILL

VERSE 2-HI-HAT REPEAT 7X   2-BAR BUILD

DOUBLE CHORUS

FILL
1.

RIDE LOOSE
2.   FILL   FILL

126

PUFFS OF SMOKE

ROGER STREET FRIEDMAN

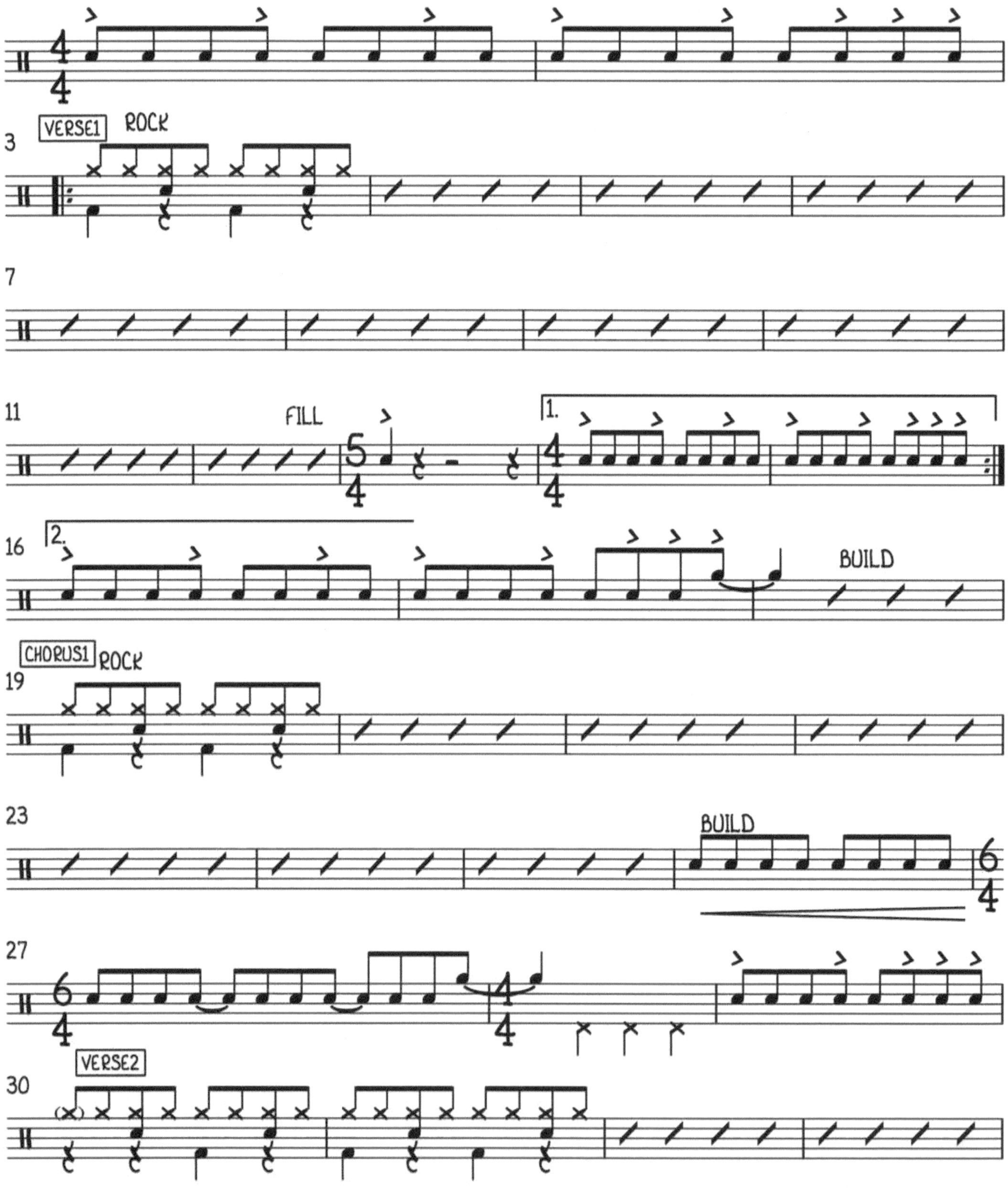

Filling In The Grooves/Extras

130

Filling In The Grooves/Extras

SHOOT THE MOON

Roger Street Friedman

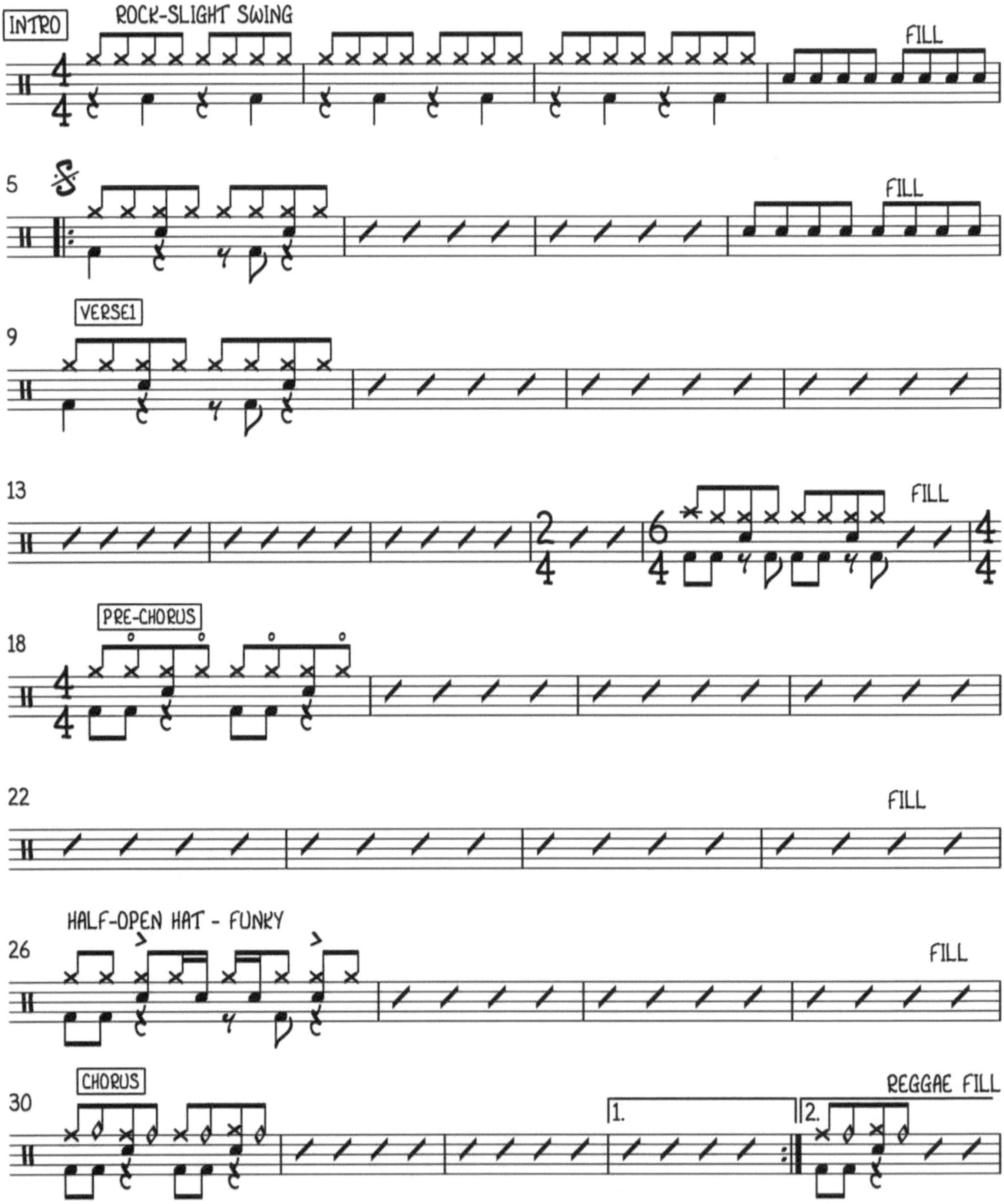

Filling In The Grooves/Extras

134

CHAPTER 11
TRIBUTE

SIMON SAYS / Simon Phillips

This page is dedicated to one of my all-time favorite drummers, Simon Phillips. I first heard Simon on Jeff Beck's *Space Boogie* and was blown away by the sheer power and excitement of his double-bass shuffle! I didn't know then the depth of Simon's playing and just how much of an inspiration he would be. His feel is unbelievable, his musicality unmatched, and if you ever meet him, his enthusiasm is contagious. Make sure you check out Simon's solo work. As a leader his material is melodic, with great rhythmic complexity at times—but always grooving. The fact that he plays open-handed is also a great testament to his dedication to the instrument. Simon is one of the pioneers in this area.

#1 "Give Blood" (Pete Townshend)

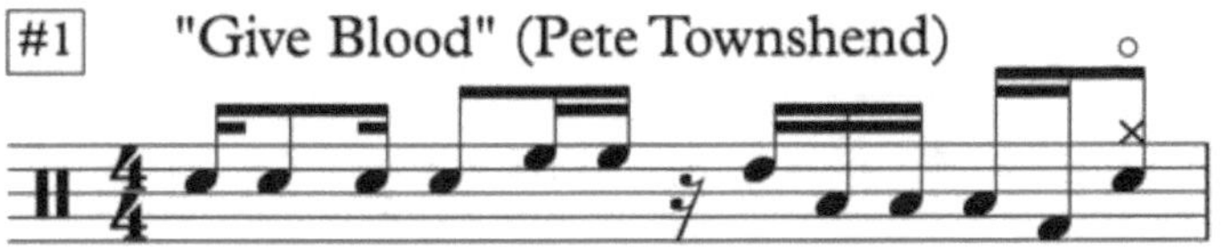

#2

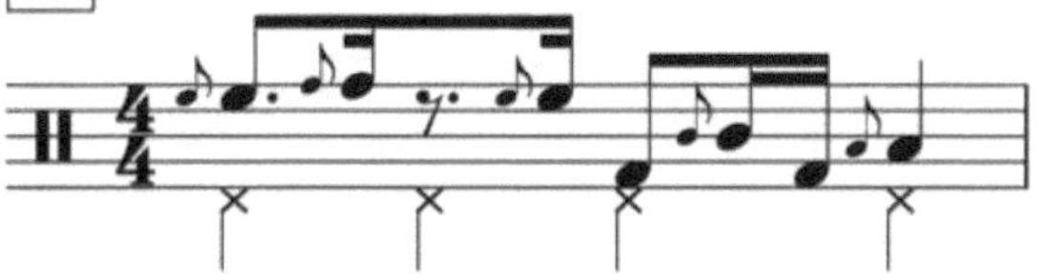

#3

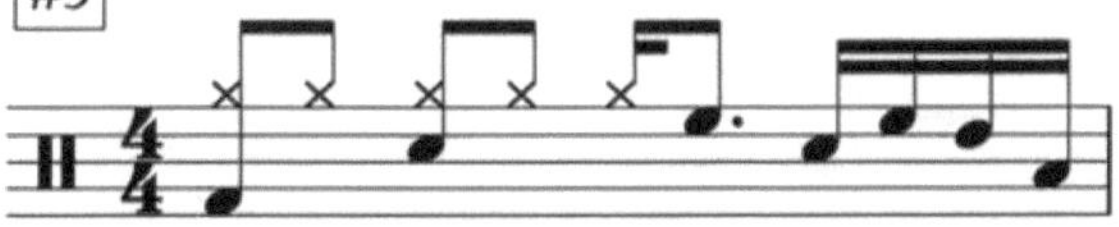

#4 "Mad About You" (Toto)

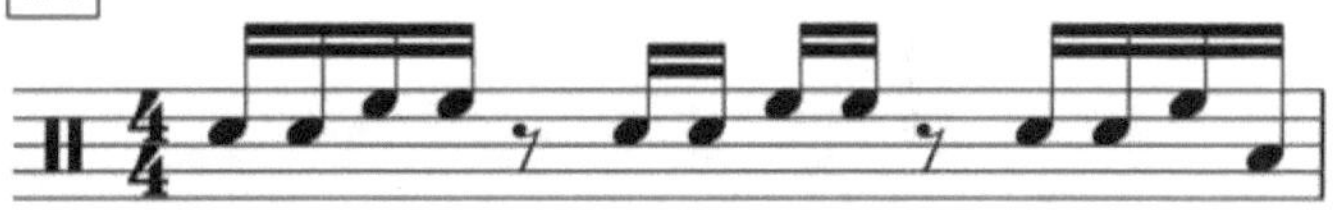

#5

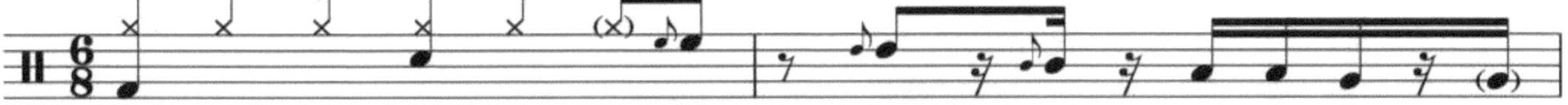

#6

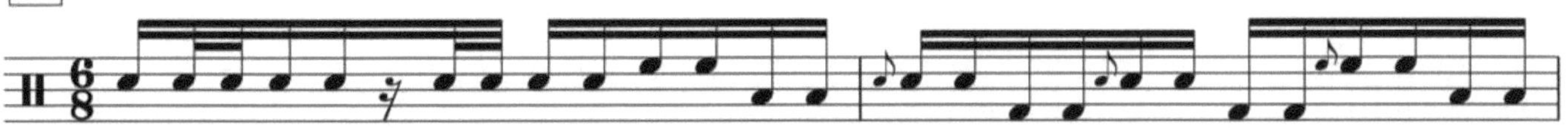

#7

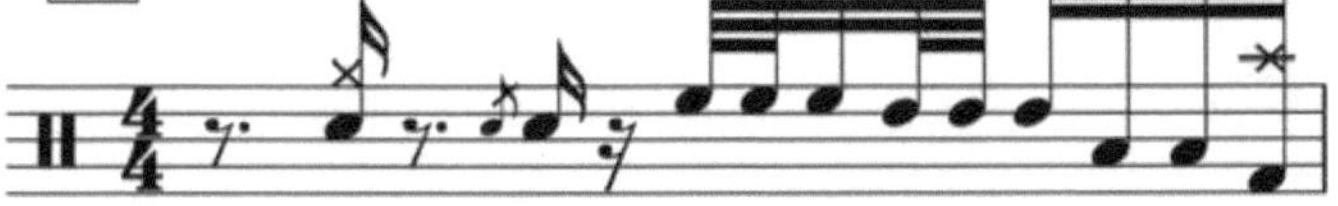

#8

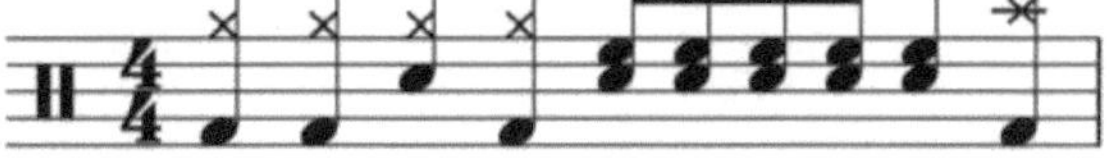

Filling In The Grooves/Tribute

GIVE ME LIBERTY / Liberty DeVitto

This page is dedicated to the great Liberty DeVitto, whose legendary career has spanned over four decades. His work with Billy Joel is unmistakable. You can always tell by his sound and style that it is Liberty playing! On tracks like "Get it Right the First Time" his musical use of the kit is dripping with originality. On "Only the Good Die Young," his brush groove is one of a kind. On "Summer Highland Falls," he plays with emotion and sensitivity. He's never about flash or chops, and his fills are tasteful and serve the songs well.

BONZO BITS / John Bonham
Iconic fills that are powerful and purposeful.

One of my earliest influences is the legendary John Henry Bonham. I can remember getting the album *Physical Graffiti* and thinking, "Wow, I want to play like that!" Bonham had raw power with serious groove, always using interesting patterns with totally intense fills. He was the whole package, and way ahead of his time! Bonham's footwork changed the way people would play rock music. When I heard "The Crunge," from *Houses of The Holy*, I knew he was even more talented than I previously thought. It's an odd-time James Brown-esque groove thing. What?! Another standout track is "Out on the Tiles," which has such interesting phrasing and is a must for any Bonham fan!

You can hear the evolution of his playing from record to record throughout his career, and it's amazing how refined his playing became by the time of the *In Through the Out Door* sessions. Legendary grooves and legendary fills: Bonzo is one of my all-time favorites!

FILL COLLINS / Phil Collins
Simple but tasteful fills played for the song.

Phil Collins has had an incredible career. He is a super-talented musician who can pretty much do it all. From his drumming with Genesis, to his fusion work with Brand X, to becoming the frontman and driving creative force in Genesis, and then having a hugely successful solo career, he is certainly one of the most successful drummers of all time. I hear drummers (especially young drummers) knock Phil Collins, but he has played drums on countless hit records, and his feel and musical sensibility make him one of the greats. His fills are there to serve the song, not to try to impress drummers. Phil's playing always makes the song work by putting every note in its place. He is one of my inspirations when I'm creating drum parts for songwriters.

"Inside Out" #1

"In the Air Tonight" #2

#3

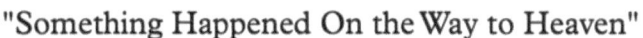
"Something Happened On the Way to Heaven"

#4

"Doesnt Anybody Stay Together Anymore" #5

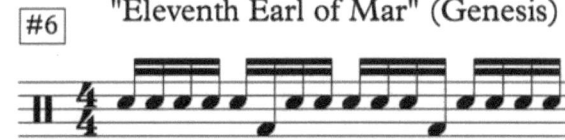
"Eleventh Earl of Mar" (Genesis) #6

"We Wait and We Wonder" #7

"No One is to Blame" #8

"Bad Love" (Eric Clapton) #9

"Bad Love" (Eric Clapton) #10

COBHAM / Billy Cobham

No funny name or pun on this page—Cobham says it all. I saw Billy play at the Blue Note in New York recently, and was humbled by his musicality. He is still playing with such joy, and his power and command over the instrument are remarkable. The first recording I heard with Billy on drums was the legendary Mahavishnu Orchestra performace at Woodstock. I was blown away by the incredible power and complexity of Billy's playing—then to find out later that he was playing open-handed! That sent me on a quest to find as many of his recordings as possible, which in turn led me to discover Billy's work as a leader. From these recordings I found that incredible pocket and groove accompanied Billy's unbelievable jazz-fusion prowess.

I transcribed some fills from Billy's solo work, which is an unbelievable flurry of notes that leaves one's mouth agape. With amazing groove, execution and musicality, Billy Cobham is still inspiring generations of drummers. He is undoubtedly one of the legends of drumming, and one of my all-time favorites.

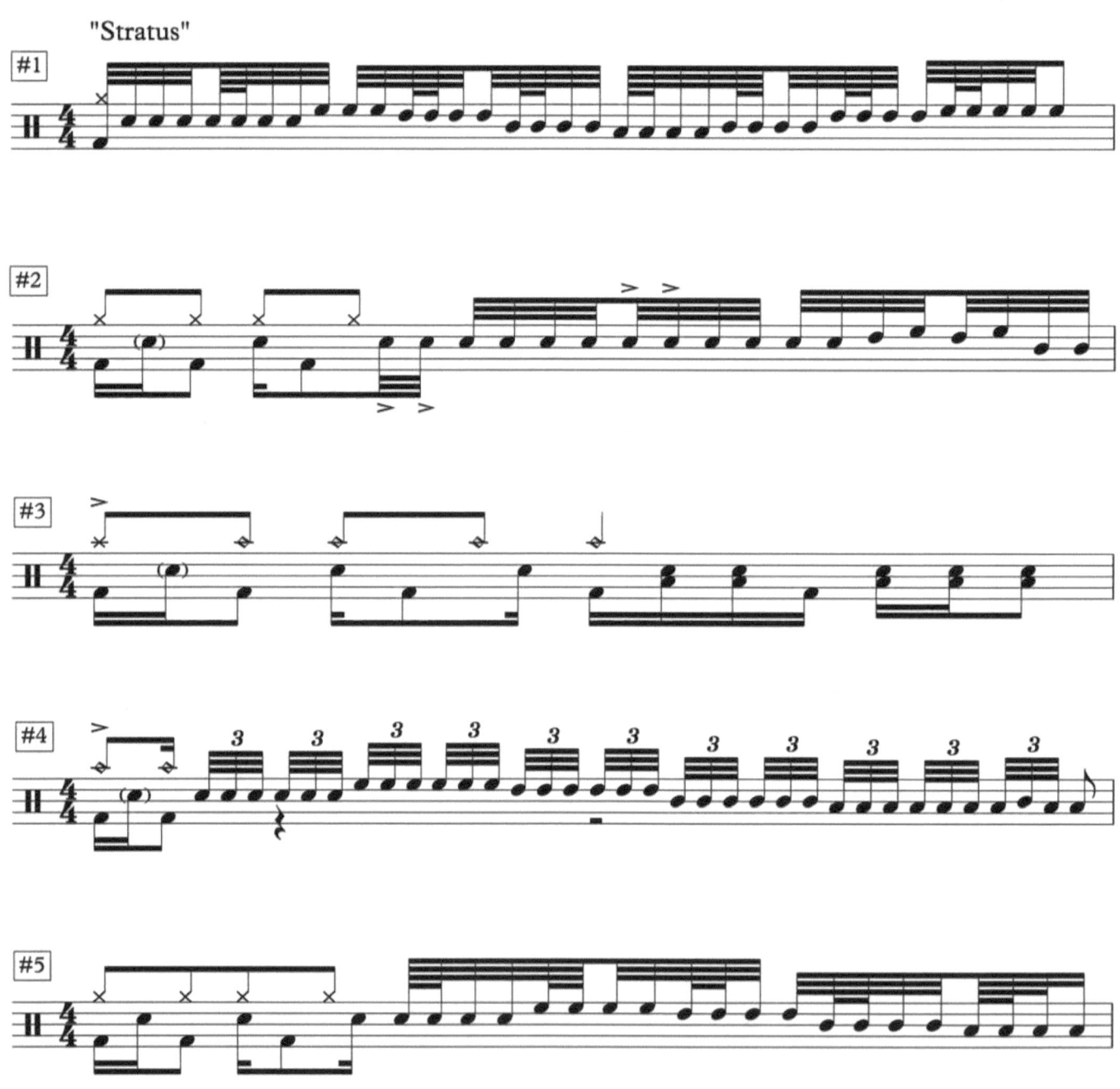

Filling In The Grooves/Tribute

SMITHTOWN / Steve Smith

Fills by one of the most important drummers of our time.

This man is a chameleon! Steve Smith is a legendary rock drummer, a fusion monster, and straight-ahead jazz professor! He sounds great on everything he does, is an expert on the history of the jazz legends, and his group Vital Information is an important part of the evolution of jazz-fusion music.

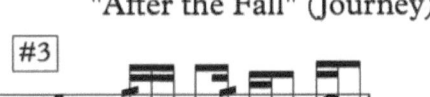

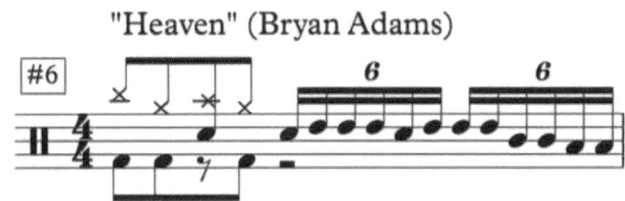

Filling In The Grooves/Tribute

JEFF PORCARO

Legendary fills that grooved as hard as his drum patterns.

If you play drums and don't know about Jeff Porcaro, you had better do your homework! You've definitely heard him, even if you didn't know it at the time. This man was a studio legend with a long discography and talent to match. Jeff Porcaro is one of those legendary musicians that people try to emulate, but no one comes close. His feel and musicality will never be replicated. Jeff's work with Toto is legendary because it feels so good!

#1 "Hold the Line" (Toto)
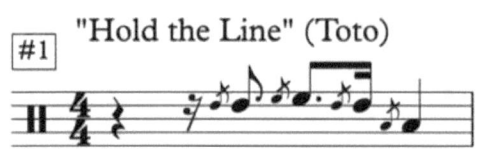

#2 "Rosanna" (Toto)
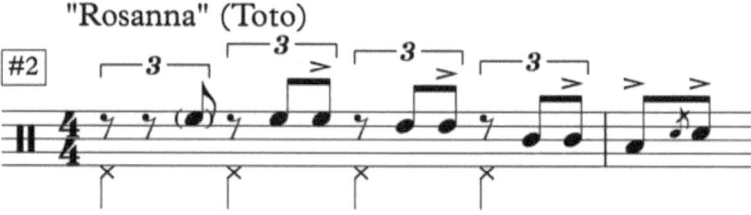

#3 "Africa" (Toto)

#4 "Lowdown" (Boz Scaggs)
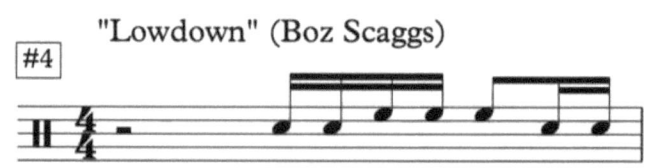

#5 "Black Friday" (Steely Dan)
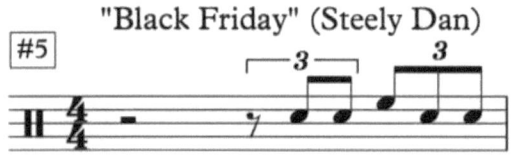

#6 "Black Friday" (Steely Dan)

#7 "How Many Times" (Toto)

#8 "Big Bone" (Los Lobotomys)

#9 "Doctor Wu" (Steely Dan)

#10 "Your Gold Teeth II" (Steely Dan)

OFFICER COPELAND / Stewart Copeland

Stewart Copeland is one of those drummers you can identify in a short sound bite by his sound and attitude on the drums. To some, his name is synonymous with the "hi-hat," because of his intricate hi-hat work on recordings from the The Police, such as "Walking on the Moon" and "Driven to Tears." Combining rock, punk, reggae, and a certain jazz sensibility, Stewart created his own unique style and sound, and is consistently named as a huge influence by many current rock drummers. Ever since I heard him in my high school years, he has been an influence and a source of inspiration!

FORGADDABOUTIT / Steve Gadd

Steve Gadd has been one of my greatest influences, from early Chick Corea to his work with Rickie Lee Jones, Steps Ahead, Steely Dan, and just about everyone else in the business! Have you seen his discography? It's pages long and organized by decade! Check out his website; it's mind-blowing just how many records Steve Gadd has played on. His feel is so relaxed, yet explosive when the music calls for it. Sophisticated with beautiful simplicity at times, Gadd can turn on a dime and blow you away with amazing technique and technical ability.

TEN STEPS TO TONY / Tony Williams
Tony's aggressive style shows he means business...

Tony Williams was a force in jazz that I regret I never got to see live. Make sure you go out and see your idols play, because they won't be around forever. I didn't become aware of just how incredible Tony Williams was until my late teens. I knew of him and had recordings, but I didn't appreciate his talent until later. His influence on the drumming world is evident in so many players, including myself. Tony was vastly musical, but had this ability to play jazz with the attitude of John Bonham. He attacked the drums, and meant every note he played. Tony was a complex musician on many levels; energetic and aggressive on fusion work with the Tony Williams Lifetime, and sophisticated and sensitive on his post-fusion recordings, like *Native Heart* and *Civilization*. These are beautifully played jazz masterpieces. Make sure you check out Tony's *Live in NYC 1989* DVD.

RINGO STARR

Fills that serve the song.

I actually came to appreciate Ringo Starr's drumming comparatively late in my studies. I was too busy listening to all of the heavy fusion and progressive rock players to appreciate the simple, yet original work of Ringo. He plays for the song—not about the drummer, but the sum of the parts. Ringo has the ability to find that perfect drum part, but it's never obvious—it always has originality and a style that is distinctly Ringo. Listen to "Ticket to Ride;" there's a groove that's not the obvious choice! When I hear young drummers say something derogatory about Ringo, I remind them of how successful his career has been, and how memorable many of his drum parts are! Originality and creativity are Ringo's hallmarks.

TODD SUCHERMAN

In addition to the drum heroes from my childhood, I wanted to talk about some drummers I think are making wonderful contributions today. Todd Sucherman is one of those drummers. His musical approach and creativity are truly an inspiration. It's evident that Todd is influenced by some of the same drummers I grew up listening to, and he has a great appreciation for the roots of drumming. Todd gives it all as the drummer for prog legends Styx, and as a world-class clinician. His DVD series *Methods and Mechanics* is as entertaining as it is educational—and it's beautifully shot! Todd Sucherman is truly an artist and a great inspiration to a new generation of drummers!

Filling In The Grooves/Tribute

#8 "One With Everything" (2:19)

#9 "One With Everything" (2nd fill) (4:30)

WHEN NEIL'S AT THE WHEEL / Neil Peart

Neil Peart is one of the most copied drummers of all time. He is truly a drummer's drummer, but also a musician's drummer, and undoubtedly the most well-known rock drummer of my generation. My mom knows who Neil Peart is! Well, she did live with me for the first 18 years of my life. Neil's legendary drum parts instill fear in students' minds when they consider learning a Rush tune for the first time. Neil Peart is the definition of originality as a drummer. He crafts his parts carefully and with intention to serve the songs, and brings forth excitement and musicality unmatched in the world of progressive rock. A compositional player, a lot of thought goes into Neil's fills, and that's why he was an obvious choice for this book! It would not be complete without him. For a great analysis of Neil's drum parts, check out Hudson Music's DVD *Neil Peart: Taking Center Stage*, and the companion transcription book by Joe Bergamini.

PORCU-TIME / Gavin Harrison
Fills by a pioneer of modern progressive rock.

Gavin Harrison is a bit of an enigma. He plays incredibly well, is meticulously detail-oriented, and has great feel and musical depth. He's an alien! I absolutely love his playing. Some of the most influential drummers in the business will attest to his skills. Neil Peart speaks highly of Gavin, and he himself seems blown away by Gavin's ability to play with time and use metric modulation on such a high level. Gavin's books and DVDs (*Rhythmic Illusions, Rhythmic Perspectives, Rhythmic Designs*) are a must-have for any serious drummer. His work with Porcupine Tree is modern and technically awe-inspiring, and his work with 05RIC is mind-boggling. A master of phrasing and use of the drum kit as a palette of sounds, Gavin's fills are filled with bursts of rhythmic complexity that are different than anything I've heard. Gavin's fills had to be included in my collection!

"Fear of a Blank Planet" (Porcupine Tree) (5:01)

R L R R L F F R L R R L F F R L R R   L F F   alternating

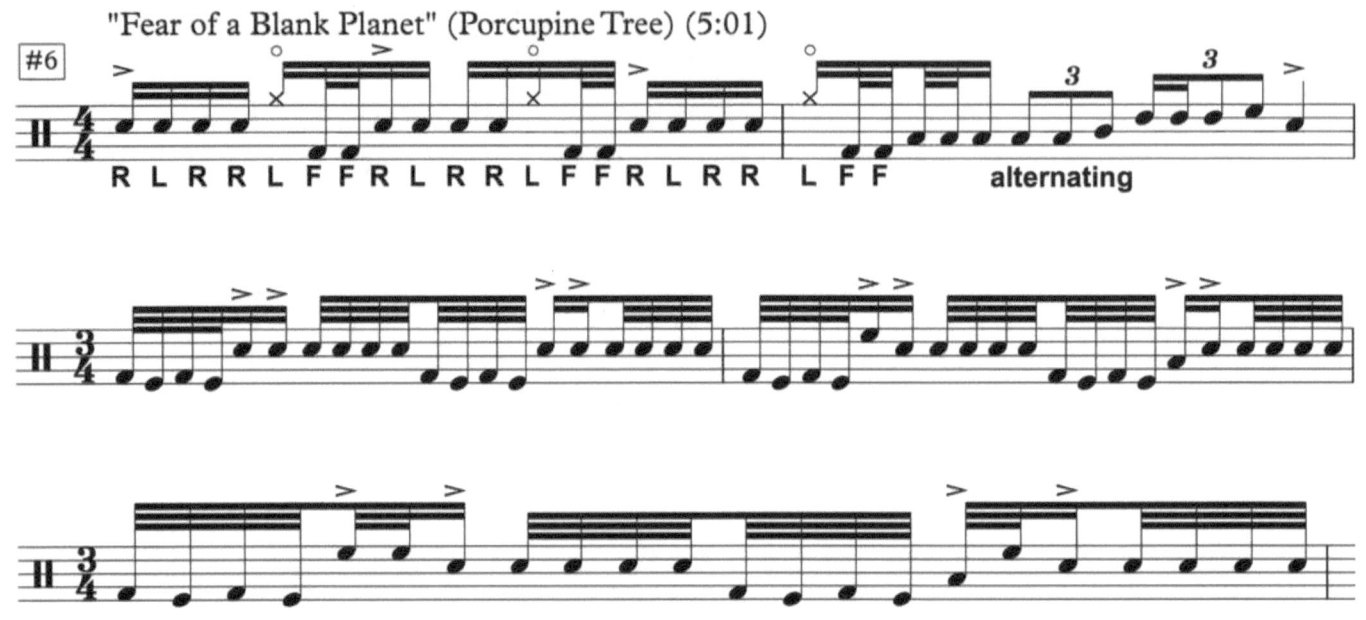

INDEX
INDEX OF PRACTICE SEGMENTS

This section contains all of the practice segments for muscle memory. Use this index to combine and form your own ideas and fills.

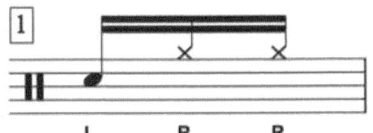
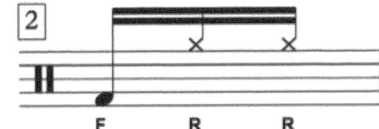
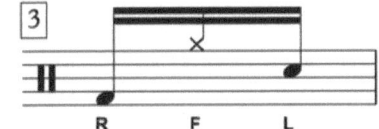

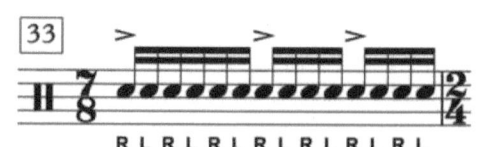

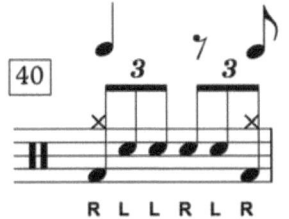

Filling In The Grooves/Index

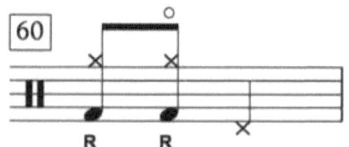

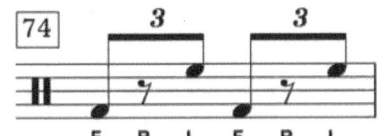

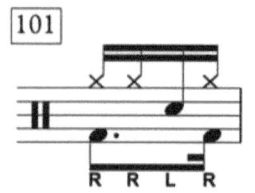
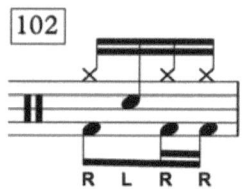
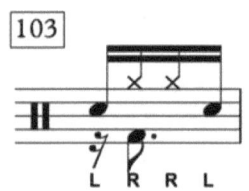

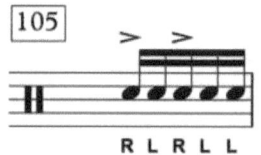

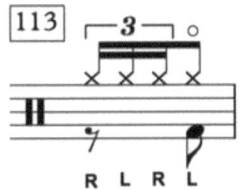
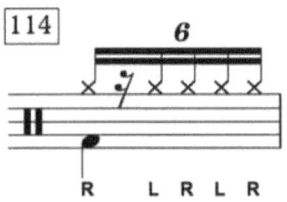

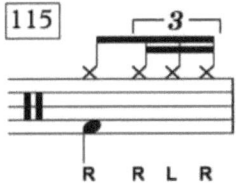

RESOURCES
Check out these materials for further study.

BOOKS

It's Your Move - Dom Famularo and Joe Bergamini
Stick Control - George Lawrence Stone
Accents and Rebounds - George Lawrence Stone
Advanced Techniques for the Modern Drummer - Jim Chapin
Four-Way Coordination - Elliot Fine
Progressive Steps to Syncopation for the Modern Drummer – Ted Reed
Survival Guide for the Modern Drummer - Jim Riley
Groove Essentials 1.0 and 2.0 - Tommy Igoe
Modern Drumset Stickings - Swiss Chris
Patterns (series) - Gary Chaffee
Rhythmic Composition, Rhythmic Designs, Rhythmic Illusions, Rhythmic Perspectives - Gavin Harrison
Steve Gadd: Up Close – Steve Gadd
Odd Feelings - Massimo Russo with Dom Famularo
Pathways of Motion - Steve Smith
The Code of Funk, Future Sounds - David Garibaldi
Open-Handed Playing 1 & 2 - Claus Hessler
Groove Alchemy - Stanton Moore
Exploring Your Creativity on the Drumset - Mark Guiliana
Turn It Up & Lay It Down: Baby Steps to Giant Steps - Peter Retzlaff & Jim Rupp
Neil Peart: Taking Center Stage - Joe Bergamini
Arrival Drum Play-Along - Joe Bergamini with Dom Famularo
Elements - John Favicchia

VIDEOS

Jim Chapin: Speed, Power, Control, Endurance
Jojo Mayer: Secret Weapons for the Modern Drummer 1 & 2
Benny Greb: The Language of Drumming
Neil Peart: Taking Center Stage
Todd Sucherman: Methods and Mechanics 1 & 2
Gavin Harrison: Rhythmic Horizons, Rhythmic Visions
Steve Gadd: Up Close
David Garibaldi: Breaking the Code
Steve Smith: Drumset Technique/History of the U.S. Beat
Simon Phillips Complete
Terry Bozzio: Solo Drums

APPS

Drum Guru
The Clave
Tempo (Frozen Ape)

RECOMMENDED LISTENING

DRUMMER	ARTIST, ALBUM
Billy Cobham	Billy Cobham, *Spectrum*
Billy Cobham	Billy Cobham, *Shabazz*
Billy Cobham	Billy Cobham, *Warning*
Billy Cobham	Billy Cobham, *Power Play*
Billy Cobham	Mahavishnu Orchestra, *Inner Mounting Flame*
Billy Cobham	Mahavishnu Orchestra, *Birds of Fire*
Chad Wackerman	Frank Zappa, *Them or Us*
Chad Wackerman	Allan Holdsworth, *Metal Fatigue*
Chad Wackerman	Alan Holdsworth, *Road Games*
Dave Weckl	Chick Corea, *Electrik Band*
David Garibaldi	Tower of Power, *Back to Oakland*
Dennis Bradford	Jeff Lorber Fusion, *Wizard Island*
Gavin Harrison	Porcupine Tree, *In Absentia*
Gavin Harrison	Porcupine Tree, *Fear of a Blank Planet*
Gavin Harrison	Gavin Harrison & 05Ric, *Circles*
Gavin Harrison	Gavin Harrison & 05Ric, *Drop*
Jeff Porcaro	Toto, *Toto*
Jeff Porcaro	Toto, *IV*
Jeff Porcaro	Toto, *Fahrenheit*
Jeff Porcaro	Toto, *The Seventh One*
Jeff Porcaro	Toto, *Kingdom of Desire*
Jeff Porcaro	Bozz Scaggs, *Silk Degrees*
John Bonham	Led Zeppelin, *all*
John Robinson	Michael Jackson, *Off the Wall*
Lenny White	Return to Forever, *No Mystery*
Liberty DeVitto	Billy Joel, *Turnstiles*
Liberty DeVitto	Billy Joel, *The Stranger*
Liberty DeVitto	Billy Joel, *The Nylon Curtain*
Manu Katche	Sting, *Nothing Like the Sun*
Manu Katche, Jerry Marotta	Peter Gabriel, *So*
Neil Peart	Rush, *all*
Ralph Humphrey, Chester Thompson	Frank Zappa, *Apostrophe*
Ringo Starr	The Beatles, *all*
Russ Kunkel	Lyle Lovett, *Joshua Judges Ruth*
Simon Phillips	Hiromi, *Voice*
Simon Phillips	Hiromi, *Alive*
Simon Phillips	Hiromi, *Move*
Simon Phillips	Hiromi, *Spark*

RECOMMENDED LISTENING

DRUMMER	ARTIST, ALBUM
Simon Phillips	Protocol, all
Simon Phillips	Simon Phillips, *Another Lifetime*
Simon Phillips	Simon Phillips, *Symbiosis*
Simon Phillips	Toto, *Tambu*
Simon Phillips	Toto, *Mindfields*
Steve Gadd	Steely Dan, *Aja*
Steve Gadd	Chick Corea, *The Leprechaun*
Steve Gadd	Chick Corea, *Friends*
Steve Smith	Journey, *Evolution*
Steve Smith	Journey, *Departure*
Steve Smith	Journey, *Dream, After Dream*
Steve Smith	Journey, *Captured*
Steve Smith	Journey, *Escape*
Steve Smith	Journey, *Frontiers*
Steve Smith	Journey, *Raised on Radio*
Steve Smith	Journey, *Trial by Fire*
Steve Smith	Vital Information, all
Steve Smith	Steps Ahead, *Steps Ahead*
Steve Smith	Steps Ahead, *Live in Tokyo 1986*
Steve Smith	Steps Ahead, *N.Y.C.*
Steve Smith	Steps Ahead, *Yin-Yang*
Steve Smith	Steps Ahead, *Steppin' Out*
Stewart Copeland	The Police, all
Terry Bozzio	Frank Zappa, *Live in New York*
Terry Bozzio	Frank Zappa, *Zoot Allures*
Terry Bozzio	Brecker Brothers, *Heavy Metal Bebop*
Todd Sucherman	Styx, *Return to Paradise*
Todd Sucherman	Styx, *Brave New World*
Todd Sucherman	Styx, *Cyclorama*
Todd Sucherman	Styx, *The Mission*
Tony Williams	Tony Williams Lifetime, *Believe It*
Tony Williams	Tony Williams Lifetime, *Emergency*
Tony Williams	Tony Williams, *Civilization*
Tony Williams	Tony Williams, *Native Heart*
Tony Williams	Tony Williams, *The Story of Neptune*
Tony Williams	Miles Davis, *'Four' & More*
Tony Williams	Miles Davis, *E.S.P.*
Tony Williams	Miles Davis, *Seven Steps to Heaven*
Tony Williams	Miles Davis, *Nefertiti*
Vinnie Colaiuta	Frank Zappa, *Joe's Garage*
Vinnie Colaiuta	Sting, *Ten Summoner's Tales*
Vinnie Colaiuta, Chad Wackerman	Alan Holdsworth, *Secrets*
Zigaboo Modeliste	The Meters, *The Meters*
Zigaboo Modeliste	The Meters, *Look-Ka Py Py*

ABOUT THE AUTHOR

Jim Toscano is a freelance drummer, educator, clinician and author in the New York City area. Playing drums since the age of 10, Jim grew up in Brooklyn, NY studying with local teachers. He then went on to study at the Drummers Collective with Kim Plainfield, Marvin "Smitty" Smith, and then with Victor Lewis and Charlie Persip at Jazz Mobile. After maintaining a busy performance schedule while working on his degree in music from CUNY's AFM 802 Music Program, Jim later found inspiration and a deeper understanding of drum technique and life from the amazing "Wizdom" of Dom Famularo. Jim has also studied with world-class drummers Marko Djordjevic, Chad Wackerman and Claus Hessler.

Jim's passion for teaching arrived at a young age. He has built a successful private teaching practice with more than 100 students, and maintains a busy clinic schedule with schools, stores, and his Hand Technique Workshop. Jim is a frequent contributor to the Sabian Education Network.

Jim has played with countless bands and artists, remaining independent, which has allowed him to constantly evolve and explore new music. Jim is currently performing with several NY artists, is involved with many recording projects, and is now in the process of producing a video lesson series for online lessons based on his on his modern drumset approach.

Jim Toscano uses Sabian cymbals, Evans drumheads and Promark drumsticks.

ABOUT THE AUDIO & VIDEO

This book includes online audio and video content. Visit www.alfred.com/redeem and enter the code found on the first page of this book. You will then be able to access this content. The video segments are organized by title, matching the chapter/section of the book. The audio content consists of numbered tracks that go in sequence from the start of the book. The track numbers match the ones included in the text.

The audio examples are downloadable MP3s of each of my own fills. The tracks are numbered to match the book. Each fill is played slowly and then in context in two four-bar cycles. Each cycle is comprised of three bars of groove and then the fill. Additionally, although this is not a "play-along" book, I have included several play-along tracks that were written specifically for this book. I hired talented musicians to accommodate the various feels and styles. You will also find an "extras" section that has tracks from sessions that I've played on where the material can be applied to real world examples.

The video files must be streamed (they are not downloadable), and are arranged into folders named for each chapter. There are video examples of many of the fills included in this book, first performed slowly and then in context with a groove as well. The video examples show the transcription and provide a visual aide into the techniques and orchestrations used on the fills. I hope you find this material both enjoyable and helpful as you work your way through the examples from the book.

FILLING IN THE GROOVES
By Jim Toscano

Edited by Joe Bergamini

Executive Producers: Dom Famularo and Joe Bergamini

Book Design and Layout by Rick Gratton

Music Engraving by Jim Toscano
Cover by Paul DiNovo
Additional editing by Dave Black
All photos and videos courtesy of the author
Photography by Michael Ellison
Video Production by Jim Toscano
Production Assistants: Stella Wu, Lauren Silverman, Michael Noto
Mix Engineers: Paul Kolderie, Vincent LaRussa, Sandra & Kamilo Kratc
Audio Recordings: Playroom Studios; Jim Toscano Drum Studio; Soundworks Recording Studio LLC, 38-01, 23rd Avenue, Suite 303, Astoria, NY 11105

MUSIC CREDITS:
"One Half Dozen" Written by Toscano / Ferrara
Guitars: Frank Ferrara
Bass: Matthew Schneider

"Something in 7" Written by Toscano / Young
Keyboards: Johnny Young
Sax Alberto: Toro

"Got The Blues" Written by Toscano / Green / Valdez
Guitar: Jason Green
Bass: Yanko Valdez
Drums: Jim Toscano

"Nawlins Style" Written by Toscano / Green / Valdez
Guitar: Jason Green
Bass: Yanko Valdez
Drums: Jim Toscano

"Shuffling Along" Written by Toscano / Green / Valdez
Guitar: Jason Green
Bass: Yanko Valdez
Drums: Jim Toscano

"Get On The Train" Written by Toscano / Green / Valdez
Guitar: Jason Green
Bass: Yanko Valdez
Drums: Jim Toscano

"Drop One In" Written by Toscano / Ferrara
Guitars: Frank Ferrara
Bass: Matthew Schneider

"Back To Basics" Written by Toscano / Ferrara
Guitars: Frank Ferrara
Bass: Matthew Schneider

"Shoot The Moon" (Roger Street Friedman Band)
Written by Roger Street Friedman
Acoustic Guitar: Roger Street Friedman
Electric Guitar: Frank Ferrara
Bass: Matthew Schneider
Trumpet: Mac Gollehon
Tenor Sax: Jay Collins
Baritone: Sax Barone Raymonde
Electric Piano: Jason Crosby
Horn Arrangement: Jay Collins

"Puffs Of Smoke" (Roger Street Friedman Band)
Written by Roger Street Friedman
Acoustic Guitar: Roger Street Friedman
Electric Guitar: Frank Ferrara
Bass: Matthew Schneider
Trumpet: Mac Gollehon
Tenor Sax: Jay Collins
Baritone Sax: Barone Raymonde
Piano: Jason Crosby
Hammond B3: Jason Crosby
Horn Arrangement: Jay Collins

"One of A Kind" (Giant Flying Turtles)
Written by Young / Bennett
Keyboards: Johnny Young
Bass: Calvin S. Bennett
Guitars: TJ Jordan

"River Runs Dry" (Giant Flying Turtles)
Written by Young / Bennett
Keyboards: Johnny Young
Bass: Calvin S. Bennett
Guitars: TJ Jordan

"Waltz to the World" (Giant Flying Turtles)
Written By Young / Bennett
Keyboards: Johnny Young
Bass: Calvin S. Bennett
Guitars: TJ Jordan

NOTES

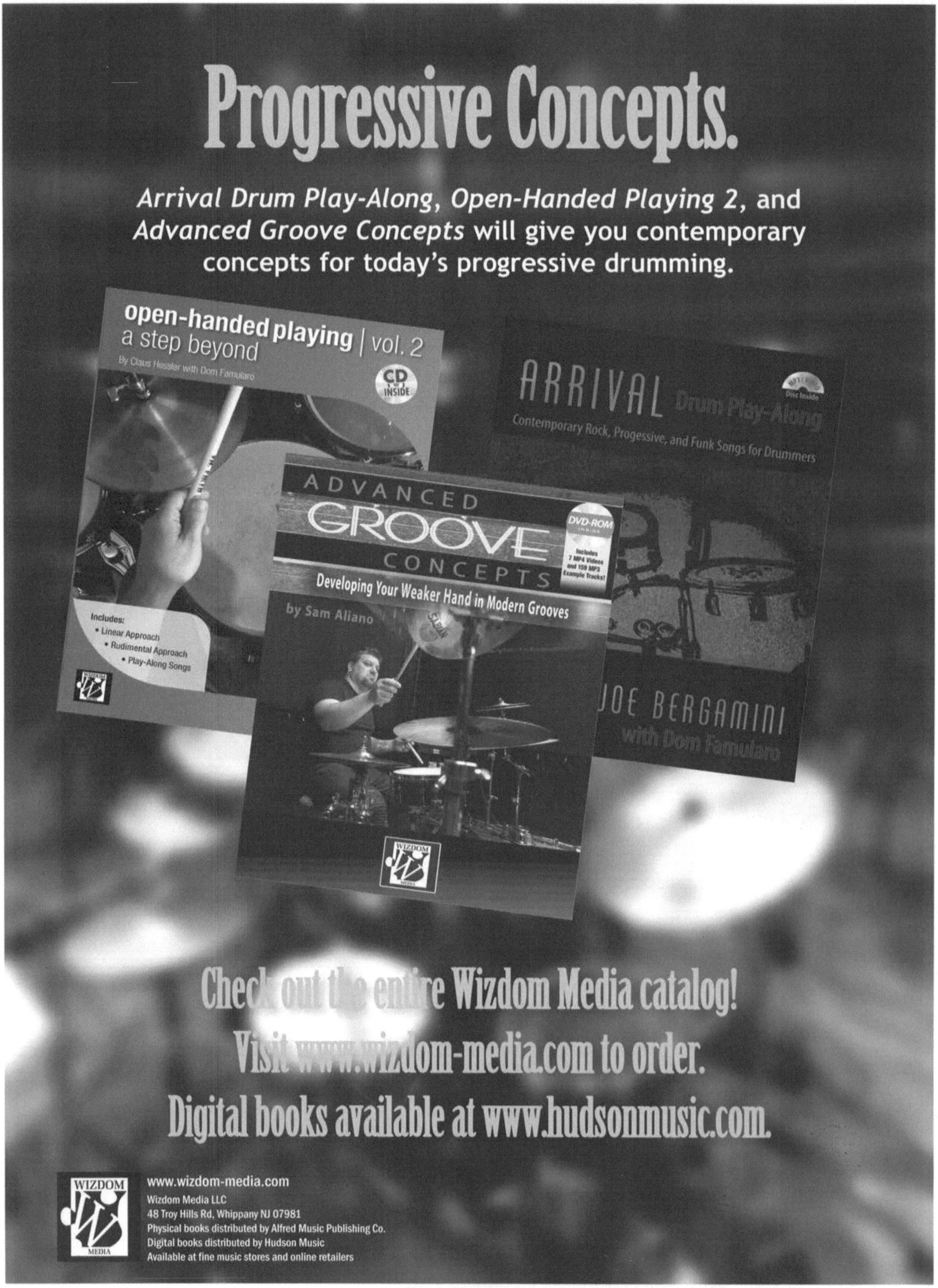

Progressive Concepts.

Arrival Drum Play-Along, Open-Handed Playing 2, and *Advanced Groove Concepts* will give you contemporary concepts for today's progressive drumming.

Check out the entire Wizdom Media catalog!
Visit www.wizdom-media.com to order.
Digital books available at www.hudsonmusic.com.

www.wizdom-media.com
Wizdom Media LLC
48 Troy Hills Rd, Whippany NJ 07981
Physical books distributed by Alfred Music Publishing Co.
Digital books distributed by Hudson Music
Available at fine music stores and online retailers